BUYING A COMPANY IN TROUBLE

To Sally

Buying a company in trouble

A practical guide

Ian E. Walker

Gower

Published by
Gower Publishing Company Limited
Gower House
Croft Road
Aldershot
Hants   GU11 3HR
England

Gower Publishing Company Limited.
Distributed in the United States by
Ashgate Publishing Company
Old Post Road
Brookfield
Vermont 05036
USA

CIP catalogue records for this book are available from the British Library and the US Library of Congress

ISBN 0 566 07289 0

Typeset by Textflow Services Ltd and printed in Great Britain by Clays Ltd, Bungay

Contents

Preface   ix

Chapter 1:   Why buy a company in trouble?   1
The strategic business plan   3
Why a company in trouble?   5
Finding a company in trouble   7
Key point summary   8

Chapter 2:   Recognising a company in trouble   9
A terminal illness   9
The external signs of a company in trouble   12
Why is the company in trouble?   14
Management problems   14
Lack of financial control   15
The 'one off' factors   16
Other factors   17
The definition of a company in trouble   18
Advice to potential purchasers   19
Key point summary   19

Chapter 3:   What are the various types of insolvency?   20
Creditors' voluntary liquidation   20
Compulsory liquidation   22
Members' voluntary liquidation   23
Administrative receivership   23
Administration order   25
Corporate voluntary arrangements   26
The level of insolvencies   26
Insolvency practitioners   27

Disqualification of directors 28
Fraudulent trading and wrongful trading 30
Transactions at an undervalue 31
Key point summary 32

Chapter 4: Should I buy before or after an insolvency? 33
Buying a company in general 33
Buying a company in trouble prior to insolvency 35
Buying a company in trouble after insolvency 37
Key point summary 39

Chapter 5: Who should advise me? 40
In-house team 41
External auditors of the purchaser 42
Specialist insolvency accountants 43
Solicitors 44
Property agents or valuers 44
Other advisors 45
Bankers 45
The pitfalls 45
Key point summary 46

Chapter 6: Should I do an investigation? 47
What investigation is required? 48
The investigation timetable 49
The statement of estimated financial position
    (or statement of affairs) 50
Key point summary 53

Chapter 7: The detailed investigation 54
General review of the business and operations 54
The previous performance of the company 55
Accounting systems 57
Accounting information 57
Company forecasts 58
Subsidiaries and other connected companies 58
Banking arrangements 59
Management 60
Employees and staff 60
Sales and marketing 61
Purchasing 61
Production/work in progress 62
Land and buildings 63
Plant, machinery, vehicles, office furniture and equipment 64
Assets under finance or rental agreements 64
Intangible assets 65
Stock 66

	Debtors	67
	Cash and investments	69
	Preferential creditors	69
	Unsecured creditors	70
	Taxation	70
	Conclusion of the investigation	71
	Key point summary	71
Chapter 8:	What about assets that do not belong to the company?	72
	Assets under finance	72
	Assets subject to reservation of title	74
	Other third-party assets	76
	Key point summary	77
Chapter 9:	What about the employees?	78
	Liabilities to employees	78
	Employees in a pre-insolvency situation	79
	Employees in an insolvency	79
	The effect of the Litster case	81
	Unfair dismissal	81
	Quantifying the potential liability	82
	Key point summary	83
Chapter 10:	What other matters should I consider?	84
	Re-use of company's name	84
	The previous directors	86
	Borrowing considerations	87
	Key point summary	88
Chapter 11:	Negotiating the offer	89
	Negotiating with the previous owners	89
	Share purchase or business and assets	91
	Negotiating with the insolvency practitioner	93
	Key point summary	98
Chapter 12:	Should I sign the contract?	99
	The parties to the contract	99
	Validity of appointment	100
	Guarantors	101
	Which assets are being sold?	102
	Caveat emptor	104
	Property	105
	The consideration	106
	Value Added Tax	107
	Books and records	107
	Other matters	108
	Completion	108
	Key point summary	109

Chapter 13: The aftermath   110
             Specific problems   110
             General strategy   112
             Key point summary   115

Appendix 1: Investigation checklist   116

Appendix 2: Proforma statement of estimated financial position   128

Index   131

Preface

'Everything is worth what its purchaser will pay for it'
Publilious Syrus (1st Century BC)
'There are more fools among buyers than among sellers'
Proverb

Bad management is said to account for 95 per cent of company failures. Failures, both corporate and personal, increase dramatically in times of recession; it is forecast that 1991 will show the highest ever number of insolvencies.

For every insolvency reported, there are even more companies teetering on the edge: they are insolvent in that they cannot pay their debts on time and, in certain cases, their liabilities will be greater than their assets, but they have yet to be pushed over the edge.

In many of these troubled companies, there is a possibility that a good core business exists which could be profitable in other hands, always provided that the price is right. But buying a company in trouble – either one that is formally insolvent or one not far off from insolvency – can be a hazardous process.

This book has been written to mitigate the hazards and risks involved in the acquisition process; to assist those directors, managers or individuals who are planning to buy a troubled company, perhaps for the first time, and where the proposed target is likely to be a small or medium sized, private company. It may also help accountants and solicitors advising the purchaser.

The book guides the potential purchaser through the various stages in the acquisition process, from the formulation of an acquisition strategy to the signing of the contract; helps the purchaser gather all the information required in order to evaluate fully the proposed acquisition; and forewarns him of the likely problems he may encounter.

The book has three main objectives: to make the purchaser aware of the risks involved so that he can take steps to minimise them; to guide the purchaser towards a full understanding of the business of the target company and of the reasons which led to the company's problems; and finally, to provide enough guidance to enable the purchaser to offer a fair price.

There is no guarantee that the purchaser's bid will be successful; if it is not, the purchaser should be able to sit back in the knowledge that someone else has paid too much. Likewise there can be no guarantee that a successful purchase means that the subsequent business will succeed. The final chapter of this book offers some suggestions on business recovery.

The book is not intended to be a definitive guide to all the accounting and legal procedures involved in the acquisition of a troubled company. Insolvent companies throw up a host of problems and I would strongly advise all purchasers to take proper advice from suitably qualified accountants and solicitors at all stages in the acquisition process.

Finally, I would like to give many thanks to Jenny Ireland for all her encouragement and assistance in editing this book. I am also grateful to Peter Henshaw who helped me with the proofreading. Any mistakes are, of course, mine alone.

Ian Walker
August 1991

1   Why buy a company in trouble?

On the surface, it is hard to see why anyone would want to buy a company in trouble. The company will have severe financial problems and a formal insolvency may well be looming or have already occurred. It is likely to have lost its market share, as well as its reputation and many of its key staff. There may be problems with the actual products or services which are supplied by the company, or in the marketing and distribution of those products. The potential problems are endless and these are only the visible defects. Underneath the surface there are likely to be many more problems; poor management and leadership, inadequate books and records, defective control procedures, and so the list continues.

Yet there may be considerable advantages to buying a company in trouble. Healthy companies offer a different set of problems to potential acquirers:

- a great deal of management time and effort will be required in finding a suitable target
- the target company must be approached with great care and tact
- the vendors are likely to be in the driving seat when it comes to negotiating the price
- there could be fundamental but hidden problems which are not revealed by the investigation but which may be the seeds of a future insolvency
- even after considerable time and expense have been expended, the final offer may be rejected
- the purchaser may be lulled into a false sense of security, may skimp on the investigation and pay too high a price
- the acquisition may prove to be too costly in terms of management time and effort with possibly disastrous results for the purchaser's original business

The solicitors acting for the purchaser in the acquisition of a healthy company will try to cover many of the potential problems with pages of warranties, restrictions and guarantees in the sale agreement. However, purchasers do not want to spend years in court tied up in litigation to try to recover an amount of money from the original vendors which may only go part of the way to compensate for the legal costs involved. Such actions will be expensive both in terms of money and management time.

Healthy companies can prove problem companies.

Take the example of a group of companies which was trying to dispose of a furniture making subsidiary which, although being reasonably profitable, did not fit in with the long term plans for the group. After courting several external purchasers, the group eventually sold the company to the existing management who had been involved with the subsidiary for several years. The small management buy-out was funded mainly by venture capitalists although the new directors did have a significant stake in the company and had provided personal guarantees in support of the company's new overdraft. The price paid was nearly £500 000.

Immediately prior to the formal sale, the company's principal customer, accounting for some 40 per cent of the turnover, withdrew its custom. The new directors continued with the purchase because they were confident that they could make good the lost sales. Immediately after the purchase, the directors decided that they had to dispose of considerable amounts of redundant stock which they did at a loss. The company struggled on for some ten months before the bank decided that it could no longer continue its support. Administrative receivers were subsequently appointed and the business and assets were eventually resold for £90 000 which was probably not far short of the true value of the company when the original purchase took place. The shareholders lost everything and the directors lost their houses when the guarantees were called in.

A purchaser of a troubled company is likely to face few of these difficulties – although some new ones do arise – provided he carries out an adequate investigation and takes proper legal and accounting advice. There are a number of possible advantages:

- the target company will be relatively easy to find
- most of the company's problems should be obvious for all to see
- the purchaser will be in the driving seat when the price is negotiated
- if a pre-insolvency offer is rejected, the purchaser may not have long to wait before he can make an offer to the receiver
- the purchaser should be able to buy the assets at a discounted price and acquire the company's business for very little
- many of the company's problems – excessive overheads, over-manning or a loss-making business segment – may already have been removed by the receiver

Troubled companies can hold hidden assets.

A manufacturer of machine tools had been making steadily increasing losses over the previous five years, principally as result of steadily decreasing turnover. The business was being managed by the grandson of the founder of the company and he had never really acquired the skills necessary to manage the company properly. He still owned most of the company's shares and, together with the other shareholders, had made several abortive attempts to sell the company. Following a particularly poor year, the company's bankers insisted on appointing accountants to undertake an investigation into the company's affairs.

The accountants reported that there was little prospect of the company returning to profitability under the existing management and that, with pressure from the company's creditors increasing every day, the business would probably start to deteriorate very rapidly. Consequently, there was a high risk that the bank and the company's other creditors would lose very much more money if the business continued. The directors reluctantly requested the bank to appoint administrative receivers to the company.

The receivers immediately reduced the workforce by half while continuing with the existing contracts. The business and assets were advertised and several potential buyers immediately came forward. Following intensive negotiations, a sale was concluded with one of the parties who had been having discussions with the directors of the company some months before the receivership. The purchaser was in the same line of business and had been looking for new premises to replace his own, which were in need of substantial amounts of money spent on them. The whole of the purchaser's existing turnover was transferred to the premises of the newly acquired business and many of the employees who had been dismissed by the receivers were re-employed. The new company is now going from strength to strength.

So acquisitions of troubled or failed companies (a more precise definition of a company in trouble follows in Chapter 2) can offer some obvious advantages. But this is not a book for asset-strippers. Certain people have made a very reasonable living out of stripping assets from troubled companies or by turning such companies around, returning them to profitability in a short period of time, before selling them on in a healthier state. But without the right skills, and such skills are rare, the acquirer is taking on a very high risk.

Rather, this book is written for those directors and managers who find themselves acquiring a company in trouble as an indirect result of a defined corporate plan, where either the potential acquisition is found to be in financial difficulties or a company in administrative receivership (or in administration or, in rare cases, liquidation) is found to fit the profile of a previously defined target.

The strategic business plan

Regardless of whether the target company is healthy or troubled, the decision to make the acquisition must arise from a strategic business plan. The preparation of a strategic business, or corporate, plan in some form or another is now considered to be essential for any company. The plan should set out in detail the various ways in which the company is going to move forward and the future strategy for the growth of the company.

The strategic plan should cover the present and future plans of the company in terms of:

- the products or services supplied by the company
- the territory into which the company sells its products or services
- the customer base of the company
- the business requirements of the company in order to achieve the above, in terms of research and development, corporate structure, manpower and management
- the likely effects on the business of competition, technological change and other outside or third party influences

The plan should assist in identifying whether the growth and expansion of the company can best be served by organic growth within the present structure of the business or, alternatively, by the acquisition of an existing company.

If the growth of the business cannot be sustained within the existing physical structure of the company, for example, where product diversification or a move to another geographical area is being contemplated, the company should consider starting an operation from scratch. But delays in getting such an operation off the ground, attaining a stage where it can become viable, or where there is evidence of strong competition in the particular area, often mean that an acquisition is the most attractive means of meeting the objectives of the business plan.

The profile of the ideal acquisition target will probably be aimed towards a company which:

- is well established
- is profitable
- has good management
- has reasonable borrowings

However there will be no incentive for the proprietors of such a business to put the company on the market. Even if they are approached and can be persuaded to consider an offer, the price required to conclude a sale is going to be relatively high.

By contrast the company in trouble can be acquired cheaply, at a discount on asset values, but will probably be unprofitable, with poor management and with excessive borrowings. The skill for the purchaser is to ensure that the deficiencies of the company are compensated for by the much lower price which is paid and that the company is capable of achieving what the purchaser intends and can return to profitability. Moreover the purchaser will want to ensure that he can turn the company round relatively quickly so as to achieve a reasonable return on capital. Otherwise he would be better off by leaving the purchase price in a building society deposit account.

One of the most important issues to bear in mind when devising an acquisition-led strategy is that of management control. For example, if the purchaser intends to expand into a new geographical area, he needs to ensure that he can control and manage the acquisition successfully from a distance. Without due consideration as to the amount of time and effort that will be required to manage the new acquisition, the result is often that either the acquired company or, perhaps more unfortunately, the original company, suffers.

In the worst case, the purchaser may find that both companies are irretrievably lost, as in the case of a small building company.

> The company had been moderately successful over a number of years in buying up old properties and converting them into flats before selling them on. Two fairly large conversions were in progress when the directors decided to acquire a small development company some two hundred miles away from their home base. The scale of the new development was far beyond the experience and capabilities of the directors and all their time was spent in sorting out problems with the new development. Within a short period of time, both companies went into liquidation, the creditors received little by way of dividend and the directors lost both their livelihoods and their homes when personal guarantees were called in.

Management control will also depend upon the new company's compatibility with the existing company or group. The degree of compatibility should be considered both at the functional level (are widgets made in the same way by both companies?) and at the control level. Any area of incompatibility will mean that more management control is required.

The quality of the existing management in the acquired company is yet another consideration. In broad terms, and leaving aside the question of compatibility, the amount of management required from the purchaser will be inversely proportional to the skills of the existing management. Of course, when one considers a company in trouble, the question of the existing management becomes all important. By definition, the company is in trouble and it is the existing management who have got the company into trouble. Any purchaser will have to consider very carefully the degree to which the existing management can be left in control of the company after the acquisition.

In certain cases, the existing management is retained only long enough for the purchaser to acquire the knowledge in the minds of such senior employees and directors. In other cases, the senior management are dismissed immediately or not taken on by the purchaser and second-tier management promoted, often with surprisingly successful results.

There are many diverse reasons why a company might wish to make an acquisition. They include:

- the acquisition of a new product or service
- the expansion of an existing operation into a new geographical area
- the elimination of a competitor
- the need for greater production capacity
- the desire to add further value to an existing product or service
- the protection of a vital supplier

Individuals may also be considering the acquisition of a company, some as a first venture into the world of business, for reasons such as:

- management buy-outs (including the purchase of a company out of administrative receivership or administration)
- semi-retirement
- roll-over relief after the sale of an existing business
- investment of redundancy pay
- as an investment for a relative

Why a company in trouble?

Many of the above reasons also apply to the acquisition of a company in trouble but the acquisition of such a company, either before or after the formal insolvency of that company, should never be the prime motivating factor behind the acquisition. At the basic level, the purchaser should view the purchase of a company in trouble as the simple purchase of a collection of assets. It should have been the intention of the purchaser, as part of a previously defined plan, to acquire a broadly similar collection of assets in approximately the same location as the troubled company. The purchaser can then carefully select the various additional available elements of the business of the troubled company until a 'package' has been built up which is most suitable and in line with the previously defined target profile.

If the fit between the target profile and the available 'package' is good, then there is justification for the purchaser to proceed with negotiations. If the fit is bad, the purchaser should think very carefully before proceeding further. In viewing the similarity between the target profile and the available 'package', the purchaser should attempt to be as objective as possible, and perhaps take advice from a third party. Such objectivity is imperative because it is often a less painful decision to coax the available 'package' into a suitable fit with the target profile than to abandon the acquisition, particularly as the acquisition is often viewed as a potential bargain.

If the purchaser views the prospect of buying a company in trouble as an instant business then, by and large, the purchase will be doomed to failure or, at the very least, the turnaround of the company will be a very long and hard struggle. Even if, as will be suggested, only the assets and business of the company in trouble are acquired, the seeds of the company's previous difficulties are all too easily acquired as well.

When considering the acquisition of a company or a business from either an administrative receiver or an administrator, it should be remembered that the target company itself may not necessarily be in trouble. Very often, and particularly with the larger insolvencies, it is a whole group of companies which is under the control of the insolvency practitioner. Individual, healthy companies may exist within the group which are not directly in either receivership or administration and the insolvency practitioner will simply be looking for a purchaser of the shares in these healthy subsidiaries.

Alternatively, these healthy subsidiaries may have had administrative receivers appointed as a protective measure, in order to safeguard the security available for the bankers of the holding company or because of intercompany guarantees for example. It is therefore important for any potential purchaser to find out exactly which companies within the group are in trouble.

There is also a further important point when considering a possible involvement with a company in trouble. In the period prior to a formal insolvency, and as part of their attempts to avoid the inevitable, the directors of such a troubled company may often try to obtain further funds for the business, either as straightforward loans or, perhaps, by offering a minority stake in the company. They might also try to sweeten such a request with the offer of a directorship. The simple advice to such potential saviours is 'Don't do it!'. To undertake such a measure, without very sound professional advice, is to take on all the problems associated with troubled companies (including shadow directorships, wrongful trading and possible disqualification) without any effective means of controlling the investment. Once the initial investment has been made, it is all too easy to get further enmeshed, with the unavoidable result that the investment is lost at the same time as the company eventually fails.

A manufacturing company had been making losses over a number of years. Investigating accountants reported to the directors and the company's bankers that there was little chance of the company returning to profitability but, at the time of the investigation, the bank was fully secured and an immediate sale of the business may have resulted in a surplus for the shareholders. The directors (who were also the company's shareholders) ignored the advice but persuaded a friend who had just sold his own business to invest in the company. The company's losses increased, the friend injected more funds and acquired a small percentage of the share capital but the bank eventually had no alternative but to appoint administrative receivers. There were no funds available for the unsecured creditors and the friend's loans were lost completely. The friend had also taken part in the management of the company and risked all the consequences of being held to be a shadow director.

Finding a company in trouble

Information about possible target companies could be drawn from any number of information sources. Such companies may or may not be currently on the market. It may be possible to identify likely candidates through internal sources available to the potential purchaser, particularly sales representatives or buyers. Other alternative sources of information available to a potential purchaser will include:

- trade associations
- business sector surveys in the financial press
- published listings
- business brokers and other specialist acquisition advisors
- banks, particularly merchant banks
- major firms of accountants

The list above may also provide ready access to troubled companies, especially those that have not yet reached formally insolvency. It is also possible that the directors of such companies will be trying actively to attract buyers through the 'Businesses for Sale' pages of the local or national press.

After a troubled company has entered into a formal insolvency procedure, the most likely acquisition sources will be through:

- an advertisement in the local or national press
- a feature in the press or on television
- purchaser already having discussions with company when insolvency occurs
- insolvency practitioners' mailing lists
- people employed by insolvent company

Within days of the formal insolvency appointment, the appointed insolvency practitioner will try to obtain the maximum possible publicity for the sale of the business and advertisements are likely to be placed in both local and national newspapers, particularly the *Financial Times* (there is an extensive 'Businesses for Sale' section in the Tuesday edition) for all but the smaller insolvencies. If the insolvency is of any significance, it is also likely to be featured on local radio or television and the larger insolvencies will be featured in the national media. Trade journals are also used by insolvency practitioners to advertise businesses for sale and there are, in addition, certain specialist publications such as *Businesses and Assets*, which deal specifically with the sale of insolvent companies.

In certain instances the directors or shareholders of the insolvent company may already be having discussions with a potential purchaser. Either the directors will have approached a likely purchaser with a view to getting rid of the company before the inevitable insolvency strikes or the purchaser will already have heard on the grapevine that the company is experiencing difficulties and will have made the approach to the directors in the hope of picking up a bargain. Occasionally, the two parties may be having preliminary discussions, blissfully unaware of the impending insolvency; the directors out of ignorance and the prospective purchaser because he has yet to start his investigation.

In many such cases, an eventual sale to the originally interested party is concluded after the formal insolvency by the appointed insolvency practitioner. The reasons are twofold; firstly, the purchaser is likely to have a genuine interest in the company if discussions have already taken place. Secondly, for the same reason, the purchaser will have a head start on any other likely purchasers.

Firms of insolvency accountants or the insolvency or corporate recovery departments of the larger firms of accountants also have a database covering all the companies which the firm is handling nationally and one of potential purchasers, either of insolvent companies in general or of particular types of assets. It is a simple matter to notify such accountants of any particular type of acquisition which is required.

One benefit of being registered on such a database is that it may be possible for a likely purchaser to be put in contact with a prospective seller prior to a formal insolvency, as a result of an investigation carried out by the insolvency practitioner. Such an investigation may have been carried out on behalf of the company's bankers, trade creditors or even directors.

In many receiverships, a sale is eventually concluded with some of the former employees of the company. Most probably such persons would include either some of the directors of the former company or some of the senior management. Such people are in an ideal position to recognise the potential for the company and to be aware of where the previous management went wrong. The biggest problem for such 'management buy-outs' is being able to raise sufficient capital for the purchase in the tight time scale in which most receivers operate.

Key point summary

- The potential purchaser should ensure that the need for an acquisition is a result of a defined business strategy.
- The purchaser should not simply regard the acquisition of a troubled company as a potential bargain.
- Do not become involved in a troubled company as a minority shareholder, as a director or as a lender.

2   Recognising a company in trouble

Unless a company fails because of a single catastrophic event such as a fire or a flood, its failure is usually a very gradual event and the seeds of such failure are usually sown years before. This chapter discusses the various stages leading to a troubled or failed company. It lists some of the outward signs of a company in trouble and examines some of the causes of failure. Potential buyers need to understand why such a company has failed. After all, the new directors and managers will not only have to tackle the problems but also ensure that they do not go on to make the same mistakes.

Many new companies fail within the first three years of their existence. If a company manages to get through this period, the accounts will usually show a period of increasing profitability and growth where current assets exceed current liabilities. A good number of companies go forward from this point and, for many directors and shareholders, the ultimate goal is a place in the unlisted securities market or even, in time, a full listing.

A terminal illness

Many companies however do not succeed and the first step is usually a decline in profitability. The directors may not be able to identify the problem because of a lack of internal controls and management accounts or because of a lack of outside help. Often the directors do not wish to pay for proper advice and they consequently tend to take on advisors of low calibre.

They may not even be aware of the decline in profitability until they discover that they require an overdraft facility for the first time or that they need more than their existing modest facility. The bank manager will talk about 'cash flow forecasts', 'a debenture', 'a fixed and floating charge' and even 'personal guarantees'. At this stage the company will probably receive the facilities it has requested but with a certain loss of pride on the part of the directors.

Following this first crisis, the company may go through a period of sales growth. But when the directors examine the monthly management accounts, they will probably notice that, for the first time, the current liabilities exceed the current assets. If management accounts are not kept, at the very least the directors will probably notice that the creditors are starting to exceed the company's debtors. They will probably realise that their customers are taking longer to pay than usual and that their suppliers are requesting payment rather sooner than they used to. By now the company is likely to be incurring losses at an ever-increasing rate. At this stage, the company has become an ailing company.

A company can often return to good health from this situation but usually not without drastic action from the directors. This may include reducing turnover or making some of the workforce redundant. It is usually not achieved without assistance from outside, for by now, most directors have become too immersed in their company's difficulties to maintain their objectivity. Crisis management is likely to become a daily, if not hourly, occurrence and, without outside help, rash decisions are probably going to be made. Nevertheless the directors are still fully in control during this period and assistance will not normally be offered unless they request it.

At this stage the company probably, strictly speaking, falls within the first definition of insolvency; that *it cannot pay its debts as and when they fall due*. The bank overdraft is likely to be at or near its limit and would probably be over the limit if all the outstanding cheques were to be presented tomorrow. The creditors are now always in excess of the debtors, especially if amounts due to the Inland Revenue and Customs and Excise are included. If the directors would only stop to think, they would realise that there is no prospect of paying for that delivery of raw materials which came in today, on the due date in 28 days time. Instead they will probably rationalise that one of the other suppliers will always be willing to wait another month or that the cheque for the Inland Revenue could be delayed. They forget, or ignore, the fact that these actions may lead to interest charges or other penalties and that the Inland Revenue or Customs and Excise may be the first to send in the bailiffs. Such matters can always be dealt with tomorrow.

The problems facing the company are now much more serious as losses continue, probably at an accelerating rate. Within a period of time, which will vary from company to company and from industry to industry, any equity which was available in the company will have disappeared. Where the company is involved in major long-term contracts and management accounts are inadequate, the failure of one of those contracts could result in the collapse of the company overnight. The company will now have fallen into the second definition of insolvency – *its total liabilities now exceed its total assets*.

The directors will probably not be fully aware of this because the definition of liabilities includes contingent liabilities, for example redundancy payments to the employees and the residual liability under leasing agreements. Furthermore, the definition of assets means that the assets should be valued at their likely realisable value and not simply the value at which they were included in the company's balance sheet, perhaps over a year ago. The freehold property which was revalued by agents a year ago at £1 000 000 and included in the balance sheet at that figure may actually, in a time of recession in the property market, only be worth £600 000. For the purpose of this book, the company is now a company in trouble.

It is usually at about this time that the writs start to arrive. The first few will probably be paid off before the matter gets to court but then it is the bailiff who has to be paid. When no cash is available the sheriff may even take walking possession over some of the finished goods or company cars and lorries or, even worse, the company's machinery may be removed to be sold at auction. It is but a short step to the arrival of the statutory demand and then the winding-up petition.

The road to insolvency

The first signs . . .

- The company needs an overdraft for the first time or is forced to increase its existing facility
- The bank takes a fixed and floating charge over the assets of the company and may demand personal guarantees from the directors
- The bank requires frequent meetings, monthly management accounts and regularly updated cash flow forecasts
- The company starts to make losses
- The company does not manage to collect its debts as quickly as it has in the past
- Current assets exceed current liabilities for the first time

. . . of a failing company

- Suppliers start to demand payment more quickly
- The bank overdraft is always at, or over, its limit and cheques are often represented
- Creditors are always in excess of debtors
- The company cannot pay its debts when they are due
- The first judgement is received by the company
- The directors delay payments to creditors wherever possible
- Total assets exceed total liabilities
- The directors start to ignore problems

Of course, many directors will never let things go this far. Instead they will take advice from their accountants and consult an insolvency practitioner about the various alternatives open to them. Alternatively, the bank manager will require an investigation into the company's affairs, again probably by an insolvency practitioner; to establish the current position of the company, as statutory or management accounts will probably be hopelessly out of date and to advise both the bank and the directors about the best way forward for the company. Unfortunately, by the time the investigation is carried out, the company's financial situation usually is such that the directors cannot continue to trade without their risking a potential liability for wrongful trading.

If advice is sought or an investigation is carried out at an early enough stage, it may still be possible to recommend drastic remedial action in order to give the company a last chance of survival. In virtually all cases though, the company will need a substantial capital injection almost immediately to remedy the excess of liabilities over assets. Without this the company will have no alternative but to begin formal insolvency proceedings.

The form of the insolvency procedure may vary from corporate voluntary arrangement or creditors' voluntary liquidation, to administrative receivership or administration. The various alternatives are described in more detail in the next chapter.

Of course when a company becomes a troubled company, its directors and shareholders may try to sell the company rather than face a formal insolvency. Such a course of action will be very appealing. Based on the above definitions, the company will be insolvent at this time and the advisors to any potential purchaser will probably advise him to wait until the company enters into whichever insolvency procedure is chosen. The purchaser can then acquire only the business and assets of the company in a comparatively clean state without being concerned either with the liabilities of the company or with any skeletons which may be lurking in the corporate cupboard. There may be extensive warranty claims by previous customers of the company or the company may be about to be sued under breach of contract.

However there may be disadvantages in waiting until a company becomes formally insolvent. In the first place the purchaser will have to cope with the various problems associated with the public awareness of a formal insolvency. The company's creditors may be reluctant to advance further credit to the new company. The company is likely to have lost at least a proportion of its customers and turnover. Secondly, an acquisition from an insolvency practitioner will undoubtedly involve bidding on the open market against competition and the purchase may not be achieved.

Buying a troubled company from the directors and shareholders is without doubt a hazardous process but the risks involved can sometimes outweigh the disadvantages of waiting until the formal insolvency. In either case, it is important for the potential purchaser to be able to recognise some of the characteristics of a company in trouble. These are dealt with below.

The external signs of a company in trouble

We have already looked at the more obvious warning signs of impending insolvency; the writs or winding-up petition. So a potential purchaser should first get his solicitor to check the appropriate registers for any winding-up petition or any writs or judgements which may be outstanding. The purchaser can also run a credit check against the company, using one of the many credit agencies, but information on smaller companies can be patchy.

Insolvency practitioners also point to less formal indicators. These, somewhat 'tongue in cheek' symptoms have included:

- a fountain in the forecourt
- a company helicopter or aeroplane

- a company racehorse (for advertising purposes)
- personalised number plates on the Porsche or Rolls Royce

There are also certain well publicised formulae for predicting corporate failure such as Altman's 'Z score'. But these are generally not applicable to the small to medium sized company.

The most readily available guide to a company's health is likely to be its statutory accounts. The major disadvantage is that the accounts on file at Companies House are likely to be at least one or two years out of date. A delay in filing accounts may be another sign of potential trouble; either the company cannot afford to have the accounts prepared or, perhaps, the accounts have been prepared but the directors are unwilling to sign them because of the picture they paint. In spite of this deficiency, a review of the accounts of the potential target will probably reveal certain key symptoms where the company is in trouble.

- **Turnover**
  Sales are likely to be decreasing, particularly if the effect of inflation is eliminated.
- **Profitability**
  If a company's accounts show an increase in turnover but a decrease in gross profit margins, the company may be trying to buy marginal sales in order to stave off the inevitable failure. In general terms, a decrease in gross profit (after adjusting for inflation) is likely to indicate potential trouble, particularly if there is also a trend of decreasing net profit or if losses are a continuing feature of the recent accounts. The net profit of the company should be analysed both before and after interest charges.
- **Net current assets**
  A company in trouble is likely to show a materially decreasing level of net current assets. A more troubled company will probably be showing a materially increasing level of net current liabilities indicating that the company may be unable to pay its debts as and when they fall due.
- **Borrowings**
  The accounts show an increase in total borrowings, such as bank overdrafts and bank and other loans, including directors' loans.
- **Hire purchase or leased assets**
  Although not necessarily of significance by itself, the fact that most of a company's fixed assets have been obtained under finance agreements may mean that the company is short of cash resources.
- **Change of bankers/auditors**
  Bankers often say that there is a far higher rate of failure of customers who have recently changed banks when compared with those who have not. Similar considerations may apply when a company changes its auditors, particularly if the change has been brought about by disagreements over dubious accounting practices or a qualified audit report.
- **The audit report**
  Is the audit report qualified on a going concern basis?

A closer examination of the company itself may reveal other symptoms. These include:

- **Loss of reputation with customers**
  The company may be losing sales and customers because of a decline in the quality of the products or services supplied or a decline in the company's after-sales service.
- **Turnover of key employees**
  A high turnover of staff at any level may indicate problems particularly if such staff are key employees.
- **Loss of market share**
  An increase in sales turnover may not necessarily mean that all is well with the company if competitors are increasing their growth and, hence, market share at a higher rate.

Why is the company in trouble?

The symptoms given at the beginning if this chapter were quite simplistic and did not explain the causes of the company's decline. Similarly, the symptoms discussed above do not show the reasons behind a company's difficulties and are only the outward signs of those underlying causes. It is important for the potential purchaser to identify the causes of the company's difficulties because he will have to tackle them if he buys the company. Here are some of the main causes.

Management problems

The causes of corporate failure are many and varied. A company may fail very rapidly for just a single reason, such as the insolvency of its principal customer. More likely though, failure will be spread over a number of years and will have its roots in a number of underlying causes such as increasing fixed overhead costs, increased competition and, perhaps, declining market demand. But failure of management is usually at the core and is cited by insolvency practitioners as the principal cause of company failure.

Broadly speaking, the various causes of a company's troubles fall into two categories; the internal factors which arise solely within the company and the external factors which are due to the effect of various outside forces. Although individual internal causes can usually be separately identified, they all fall within the control of the company's management. And even certain external causes of difficulty can have their effects reduced by good management. Strategic management errors include:

- **Lack of management experience and depth at board level**
  In many smaller companies, there are likely to be only one or two active directors, who will also be the company's principal shareholders. If the company has managed to survive its first two or three years, the directors will have acquired a certain ability to manage the company but it will probably be biased towards their own backgrounds, usually either sales or production.

● **Unwillingness to fill skill gaps or engage high calibre professional advisors even though the directors acknowledge that they lack certain management skills.**

Here, the directors are unwilling to spend money on activities which they regard as incidental to the principal aim of the company. As the company grows, it will become even more important to have a breadth of skills at board level but, by then, the existing directors are unwilling to give up part of their company in order to appoint suitably qualified directors.

● **The managing director is autocratic**

An autocratic managing director can offer a certain strength to the management team but where the managing director refuses to change or to take advice from other board members, the board becomes totally ineffective. The autocrat is also more likely to gather around himself a board which is unlikely to challenge his decisions and powers, rather than for any sound business reason.

● **Concentration on new business to the detriment of the original business**

Diversification may well be necessary for the survival of the company if the original business has reached a stage where it is no longer viable. Even so, the core may still need to provide cash flow for the new enterprise. The risk is that new ventures will be pursued with vigour simply because the management has become bored or complacent with the original business and any failure to manage the original business properly can lead to the failure of the whole company. Such neglect can often be seen where the new enterprise is located at some geographical distance from the original company and the management is therefore absent in body as well as in mind.

● **'Things will change next year'**

Lack of management skills is very apparent in companies which have sustained losses for a number of years, where the directors constantly expect that 'things will change next year'. Cash flow and profit forecasts showing a dramatic turnround in the company's fortunes 'next year' are also typical. In some cases, there may be large injections of loan capital, from the directors and associated individuals, which are required in order to fund the continuing losses since the company's bankers have long since declined to increase the overdraft facility. In the worst cases, the final tranche of loans will have been injected into the company only days or weeks before its failure.

● **The failure to prepare for what are now regular down turns in the economic cycle.**

Recessions are now a regular feature of the British economy. The prudent director should be prepared for these down-turns in the economic cycle and he should have built up and retained reserves within the company wherever possible. During recessionary periods he should not hesitate to scale down overhead costs to match the decline in the company's turnover.

Lack of financial control

Insolvency practitioners will probably give lack of financial control as the second most popular reason for the failure of companies and, again, it is invariably a direct result of poor management. The lack of control is often evidenced by an absence of any form of management accounting information or by a lack of any form of costing system. In other cases, the management information or costing systems need a major overhaul in order to provide meaningful and useful results.

It is surprising how many smaller companies, and some that are not so small, are managed solely by the 'seat-of-the-pants' method with little or no management accounting information being provided to the directors. When the company is growing and the economy, in general, is prospering, the method may not present any problems. However, as soon as problems start to set in, the company's management usually has little or no idea as to precisely what the problems are and almost arbitrary decisions are taken in order to try to improve the situation.

At the other extreme, some management information systems, particularly those which are computerised, will produce such a plethora of paperwork that little meaningful information can be extracted. A side effect of such systems is that the information can take a long time to become available so that it is hopelessly out of date by the time it is eventually received by the directors.

In order to be satisfactory, the financial information provided to the company's management should be simple, effective and produced on a timely basis. In any company with proper control procedures, there is no reason why approximate monthly management figures should not be available within four or five days of the month end with accurate results being available within a further week. In the case of a company in trouble, of course, certain key data will be required on a daily basis.

In a manufacturing business, inadequate management information is likely to be the result of an ineffective, or absent, costing system. There are many instances of failed companies where the management was almost unaware of the true costs of manufacture until the financial accounts had been prepared, often months after the year end. This led to the commencement of unprofitable contracts, or the continuing manufacture of unprofitable products, leading to the eventual failure of the company.

The 'one off' factors

It is very easy for a company to start to experience difficulties either when embarking on single, large projects or when it is overly dependent on a single customer or supplier. Specific examples would include:

- a move to new premises either with underestimated or inappropriate funding in place
- underestimating the costs involved in setting up the manufacture and launch of a new product line
- paying too much for an acquisition
- taking on a single, large contract of a type or in an area in which the company has little previous experience
- being reliant on a single supplier who is able to increase the price of materials which, in a competitive situation, cannot be passed on to customers

- being reliant on a principal customer who is able to control the price at which goods are sold to him
- being reliant on a principal customer or supplier who fails

Other factors

There are a variety of other causes of potential troubles for a company. The following list is not intended to be exhaustive nor is it necessarily in any order of importance.

- **Inappropriate funding**
  This is the classic use of long-term funds for short-term purposes; the use of an overdraft to buy a freehold property instead of a term loan or mortgage or the use of an overdraft to fund speculative research and development projects instead of equity capital.

- **Lack of reinvestment in new plant or technology**
  Particularly in certain 'high tech' or highly competitive industries, a company must continually be looking to improve its product or product range. Similarly, almost all products have a natural life. Towards the end of this natural cycle, new replacement products will have come into being, usually produced by a company's competitors. The manufacturer of the original product must either adapt and diversify or fail.

- **Lack of credit control**
  Many companies consider that there is little further to be done once a sale has been made and, as a consequence, have far too much valuable money tied up in debtors. They do not consider the financial effect of either selling to poor credit risk customers or, simply, not collecting in debts for many months. The problem can be exacerbated where a company's overdraft is limited by a calculation based upon the level of debtors. In such a situation and where the company is going through a difficult period, there is little incentive for the company to collect in its debts.

- **Poor distribution or sales force**
  Most companies cannot afford the luxury of simply sitting back and waiting for customers to come to them. The product has got to be advertised, an effective sales team employed and the product must be distributed to the customers. A deficiency in any of these areas will ultimately cause problems.

- **High costs**
  A small company producing 1 000 widgets a week is unlikely to be able to compete with a much larger company, just down the road, producing 100 000 widgets each week. There will be economies of scale both in terms of the purchasing power of the larger company and in the absorption of overhead costs. It is also too easy to lose control of overhead costs (and directors' salaries and other benefits) which must be tailored to fit the gross profit being generated.

- **High stock levels**
  The management of a company can easily ignore the amount of money which

is tied up in high levels of stock and the extra interest which is being charged as a result. Stock levels should be checked regularly and surplus stocks should be disposed of, at a discount if necessary.

- **Inefficient production**

  A company producing individual order quantities of ten widgets, with a high machine downtime between each order, will obviously be less efficient than a company which produces 100 widgets in each production run. Similarly, a company supplying 100 different product lines is likely to be less efficient than a similar company which only supplies a basic ten lines, if only in terms of stock holding costs. Inefficiencies in production may also include:

  - poorly maintained plant and equipment
  - an inefficient layout of the factory
  - an inefficient labour force

- **Overtrading**

  Again this is a classic situation where a company's turnover simply grows too quickly and where there is insufficient working capital to sustain the growth. Overtrading as such may not be a potential problem where sufficient funds are available but, if the growth in sales has only been achieved at the expense of gross margin, it is probably that the company will soon be experiencing difficulties. Where the sales growth increases at a very rapid rate, the company may find that its administrative procedures cannot cope with the extra work and chaos can soon follow.

The definition of a company in trouble

We have looked at the simple case of a company that is clearly in trouble and which is about to enter a formal insolvency. We have also looked at some of the symptoms and underlying causes of company troubles in general. For the purpose of this book, a company in trouble is defined as an insolvent company, whether or not the company has already entered into formal insolvency procedures, and it is most likely that our company in trouble will exhibit a number of underlying causes of its insolvency.

It should be stressed that the company is not simply 'going through a difficult patch' but that it falls within one or both of the two definitions of insolvency in that:

- it is unable to pay its debts as and when they fall due
- it has insufficient assets to meet all the claims of its creditors, including contingent or prospective creditors

In general terms, a company is likely to fall initially under the first definition of insolvency when the level of trade creditors exceeds the combined total of debtors and available bank funds. As matters deteriorate and losses continue, the company will gradually absorb any potential surplus which may have been available in its fixed and other assets until there will come a point in time when the company also falls under the second definition of insolvency.

It is important to note that this point will be reached some time before the total liabilities exceed the total assets from a strict accounting viewpoint because, under the second definition of insolvency, it is necessary to include liabilities which are not normally shown in the company's accounts, such as redundancy payments to employees and residual liabilities under leasing or rental agreements. Moreover, the valuation of assets should be stated as being the value which they will achieve upon realisation and this is likely to have a further negative effect on the net assets position, when compared with the statutory accounts of the company.

Advice to potential purchasers

As far as the potential purchaser of the company in trouble is concerned, it is suggested that, when the target company falls within the first definition of insolvency and cannot meet its debts as and when they fall due, the purchaser *may* consider either the purchase of the company, or the purchase of the business and assets of the company, from its existing shareholders.

If the target company has reached the second definition of insolvency, there can be almost no justification for the purchaser to consider the purchase of the company as a whole from its existing shareholders. Quite apart from any consideration which will be paid for the shares, the purchaser will immediately have to inject funds in order to restore the company to solvency, on an assets basis, together with further funds in the form of working capital in order to ensure that liabilities can be paid for as and when they fall due. However, it might be possible for the purchaser to consider the acquisition of the assets and business of the company at this stage and this will be discussed in Chapter 4.

In most cases though, once the target company has reached the second definition of insolvency, the purchaser should be advised to wait until the company enters into one of the formal insolvency procedures and then to acquire the business and assets of the company from the appointed insolvency practitioner. It is the various insolvency procedures which are discussed in the next chapter.

Key point summary

- For the purpose of this book, a company in trouble is defined as an insolvent company.
- Prior to a formal insolvency, a company in trouble is likely to exhibit many symptoms of difficulty and have many underlying causes.
- The most significant cause of a company's difficulties is likely to be management problems.
- If a target company's liabilities exceed its assets, the potential purchaser should be advised, in general, to defer any question of purchase until after the formal insolvency of the company.

3   What are the various types of insolvency?

We have now looked at some of the advantages, and a few of the pitfalls, of buying a company in trouble. We have also looked at the various causes of company failure. This chapter looks at the various types of corporate insolvency and some of the problems which may arise in dealing with insolvent companies. The question of personal insolvency, either bankruptcy or individual voluntary arrangement, will not be considered.

Creditors' voluntary liquidation

A creditors' voluntary liquidation usually starts with instructions from the company directors to an insolvency practitioner directing him to call meetings of the members and the creditors of the company. A period of some two to three weeks will usually elapse before such meetings are called and, during this hiatus period, the directors remain responsible for all aspects of the company's affairs. During this period, the directors will usually be guided in their actions by the insolvency practitioner. It is likely that they will have been told, for example, that they should not incur any further credit unless it is absolutely necessary and will serve to enhance the value of the company's assets.

Immediately after receiving instructions from the directors, the insolvency practitioner will send notices to all the shareholders and creditors of the company giving them notice of the forthcoming meetings. On behalf of, and with the assistance of, the directors, the practitioner will then prepare a report on the history of the company and the various matters leading up to the liquidation, together with a statement of the company's affairs, for submission to both meetings.

At the shareholders' meeting, two resolutions are normally passed; firstly, that the company should be placed into creditors' voluntary liquidation and, secondly, that a person be appointed as liquidator of the company. In most cases, the person appointed as liquidator by the shareholders will be the insolvency practitioner who was first consulted by the directors of the company.

The shareholders' meeting is customarily followed immediately by the meeting of the company's creditors. It is at this time that the creditors have an opportunity, and normally their only opportunity, to put questions to the one or more directors of the company who will be present. It is mandatory for a director to act as chairman of the meeting of creditors although most of the chairman's duties will probably be taken over by the liquidator who will be assisting the chairman in the running of the meeting.

The most important function of the creditor's meeting is to appoint the liquidator of the company. This will be achieved either by ratifying the choice of the shareholders or by appointing someone else. If the choice of liquidator proposed by the shareholders and the creditors is different, the matter will be decided on by taking a vote at the meeting of creditors, with creditors' votes, cast either in person or by proxy, being determined solely by the size of their debt.

The liquidator has a limited ability to dispose of a company as a going concern. Principally, this is because his powers to continue the trade of a company in liquidation, as defined by the Insolvency Act 1986, are such that he can only continue the business of a company so far as it may be necessary for its beneficial winding up. Furthermore, if a liquidator does continue the trade of a company, he is trading in his own right and claims for damages will fall against him personally. In practice, trading in a voluntary liquidation is usually limited to the completion of certain contracts or work in progress, for example. Most potential purchasers of such a business would maintain that any likely goodwill of a company has disappeared upon its liquidation. It is therefore probable that a liquidator will only continue the business of a company if he can be certain that, to do so, will enhance the value of the assets being sold. Alternatively, it may be that limited, continued trading will increase the dividend paid to creditors because creditors' claims for damages under breach of contract can be reduced.

Occasionally a situation will arise where the directors have found a purchaser for the assets and business of a company prior to the liquidation. If such a transaction were to be concluded before the liquidation, the creditors' meeting will usually be stormy with allegations of sharp practice and sometimes fraud. In such cases, it is preferable to delay the sale until immediately after the creditors' meeting. This point should certainly be borne in mind by potential purchasers of the business and assets. Even though a pre-liquidation purchase may have been completely above-board, it would be all too easy for the purchase to be tainted by allegations which come to light at the creditors' meeting, even though such allegations may be groundless.

> Several years ago, before the implementation of the Insolvency Act 1986, the liquidation of a road haulage company took place. The directors of the company who were present at the creditors meeting were notorious for acquiring troubled companies, extracting as much as they could from the companies by way of assets, management charges or directors' fees, and then putting the companies into liquidation. The creditors' meeting room was packed with irate creditors, and members of the press, who expressed much concern at the sale of the company's business only a few days before the meeting.

The subsequently appointed liquidator, who ousted the shareholders' nominated liquidator, investigated the sale and found that a reasonable value had been obtained. However because of the comments in the press immediately after the creditors' meeting, the customers and creditors of the new company were very reluctant to deal with it. This led to a shortage of working capital in the new company and a hard struggle for survival. The difficulties would probably have been reduced if the purchaser had waited to conclude the sale with the liquidator.

The potential liquidator can obtain valuation advice during the hiatus period to demonstrate that the sale is at a fair and proper price and the sale can then be subsequently approved by a meeting of the liquidation committee held immediately after the creditors' meeting. However, the liquidator will have to prove to the liquidation committee that he has obtained the best price for the assets and business of the company. By their nature, the negotiations will probably have been conducted with only one interested party and it may be difficult to prove in such circumstances that a true open market price has been obtained. The liquidator may consider that he has to undertake a limited advertising campaign although, with a potential purchaser already available who may not be inclined to hold his offer open indefinitely, the advertising will have to be carried out swiftly and may only serve to confirm the price already offered, rather than being a genuine invitation to buyers.

Compulsory liquidation

A compulsory liquidation is a winding up of a company by order of the court. The petition for the winding up may be presented by the company itself, the directors of the company, one or more shareholders, one or more creditors or by an administrative receiver or administrator of the company. The most common grounds for the presentation of a petition are either that the company is unable to pay its debts or that it is just and equitable for the company to be wound up. In the latter case, it is not necessarily a prerequisite that the company is insolvent. However, in the vast majority of cases, the petition is presented by a creditor because the company is unable to pay its debts. The presentation of the petition will usually have been preceded either by a court judgement against the company by the creditor or by the creditor having served a valid statutory demand upon the company which has remained unsatisfied for the required period of 21 days.

There are provisions within the insolvency legislation for the business of a company to be continued, in the period between the presentation of the petition and the making of a winding up order, by means of a provisional liquidator and a special manager. Indeed, once a liquidator has been appointed, the liquidation committee can sanction the continued trading of a company. However, the compulsory liquidation of a company is usually the end of its business. The directors should have adopted other insolvency procedures, prior to the compulsory liquidation, if they had wished to maximise the realisable value of the company's assets in a sale of at least part of the business. By the time a petition is presented, there is often little left for a liquidator either in terms of business or assets and, in many cases, the bailiffs will have removed most of the company's goods prior to the liquidation. As a consequence, businesses are rarely sold by compulsory liquidators.

Members' voluntary liquidation

A members' voluntary liquidation is instigated when the directors and shareholders consider that the affairs of a company should be brought to a close because no useful purpose can be served by the company's continued existence. The procedures are broadly similar to those involved in a creditors' voluntary liquidation but with one important difference; in a members' voluntary liquidation, the directors of the company must swear a declaration of solvency to the effect that the company will be able to pay all its debts, together with interest, within a period of not more than 12 months.

The reasons for commencing a members' voluntary liquidation can be many and varied. They range from a simple distribution of cash to shareholders at the end of a company's life to the disposal of an unwanted subsidiary by a parent company. Whatever the reason, the fact that the company is ostensibly solvent means that, for our purposes, it is not a troubled company. If during the liquidation, the solvency of the company is called into doubt, the insolvency legislation contains procedures for converting the liquidation into a creditors' voluntary liquidation.

Administrative receivership

The appointment of an administrative receiver, or more usually, joint administrative receivers, to a company can only be made by the holder of a debenture secured by a floating charge. Prior to the implementation of the Insolvency Act 1986, an administrative receiver was known as a receiver and manager. An administrative receiver is appointed over the whole, or substantially the whole, of the assets of a company. This contrasts with, for example, a receiver appointed by a mortgagee over a specific property under the Law of Property Act 1926. In practice, an administrative receiver is often appointed to a company by a bank, which has lent money to a company secured by a debenture giving the bank a fixed charge on any properties owned by the company, and usually the debtors of the company, together with a floating charge over the other assets of the company.

When a bank is having problems with a company, perhaps because of a lack of up-to-date information, cheques being presented which would take the company's overdraft over its facility level, or a request from the company for further funds where the bank is not happy with the level of security available, the bank may request the directors of the company to allow the bank to appoint investigating accountants. Their job is to prepare an independent report for the benefit of both the directors and the bank. If investigating accountants are brought in to a company at an early enough stage, the report may make recommendations which, if followed by the directors, may allow the company to remedy any problems it may be having. The investigating accountants may then be required to monitor the progress of the company over a period so as to ensure that the recommendations are being followed.

In many cases, unfortunately, the investigating accountants find that there is no alternative but to recommend that the company enters into a formal insolvency. If there is no business left to dispose of, they may recommend that the directors have no alternative but to commence proceedings for voluntary liquidation. Usually, however, the accountants will be able to identify at least a core business which they consider could be sold as a going concern. This would enhance the value of the company's assets by ensuring the continuance of that part of the company's business, while also ensuring employment for at least some of the workforce.

A principal part of the investigation process will involve the preparation of a statement of affairs. An example of such a statement is shown in Appendix 2 (see page 129). The important part of the statement is that it includes estimated values for the company's assets and liabilities on both a going concern basis, which assumes that at least part of the business can be sold as a going concern, and an underlying security or forced sale basis. The latter attempts to estimate what the value of the company's assets and liabilities would be if the business were to close down immediately with a sale of assets by auction, for example. The difference in asset values on the two bases is an indication of the value of the goodwill attributable to the business as a going concern. Such goodwill is rarely shown as a separate heading in the statement, merely as an enhancement in the value of the assets. It is important to note that the term 'going concern' in these situations does not refer to a sale of the whole company, including all the liabilities, but rather the sale of certain assets of the company, including the goodwill, such that at least part of the business continues as a going concern.

Where investigating accountants find that the company has no alternative but to proceed with formal insolvency proceedings, but that at least part of the company's business can probably be saved, it is likely that the accountants will recommend the appointment of an administrative receiver, where such an appointment is possible. This is likely to be where there is a bank which has a debenture secured by a floating charge and where the bank is owed sufficient monies to justify such an appointment. If the bank then accepts the recommendations, it will usually invite the directors to request the bank to make such an appointment. The appointed administrative receivers are usually partners in the firm of accountants who undertook the investigation. The appointment is normally made quickly and, once the administrative receivers have accepted their appointment, they are totally responsible for the day-to-day business affairs of the company.

The powers of the administrative receiver are very wide and are detailed in the Insolvency Act 1986. They include the powers to take control of and to sell assets, to form subsidiaries and to hive down assets to such subsidiaries and to carry on the company's business. Moreover, until the company goes into liquidation (which can happen during the course of the receivership), the administrative receiver acts only as agent of the company. Obviously, he can be personally liable for negligence and similar offences but, in general, the liability of an administrative receiver is limited to the value of the assets in the company under his control.

The powers available to an administrative receiver enable him to continue to trade a company for a period of time, in order to sell the business and assets of the company as a going concern, and thus to realise the best possible price for those assets. Consequently, where the purchase of the business and assets of an insolvent company is being considered, purchasers will most likely be dealing with an administrative receiver.

Administration order

The concept of the administration order was introduced by the Insolvency Act 1986 but, with the exception of certain well publicised examples such as Polly Peck and Sock Shop, the procedure has not been widely used since its introduction. The original purpose of the procedure seems to have been threefold:

- to give a company in difficulty a breathing space to sort out its affairs
- to give an insolvent company, where at least part of the business could survive, a chance to achieve a going concern sale similar to a receivership but where either no debenture holder exists or the debenture holder is unwilling to appoint an administrative receiver
- to take advantage of the powers available to an administrator which, although similar to those of an administrative receiver, include additional powers such as the power to appoint directors and the power to sell charged assets

The procedure starts with an application to the court for an administration order. The application may be made by the company, its directors or one or more creditors. Before making such an order, the court has to be satisfied, firstly, that the company is, or is likely to become, unable to pay its debts and, secondly, that the making of an order would be likely to achieve one or more of the following purposes:

- the survival of the company, or at least part of its business, as a going concern
- the approval of a voluntary arrangement
- a more advantageous realisation of assets than would be achieved in a liquidation
- the sanctioning of a scheme of arrangement under the Companies Act 1985

Assuming that the court is satisfied, it may then grant an administration order which prevents any further action being taken against the company. It also prevents a debenture holder who is entitled to do so from appointing an administrative receiver. For this reason, and because such a debenture holder must be given notice of an application for an administration order, most debenture holders would usually prefer to take the opportunity to appoint an administrative receiver rather than let the administration order proceed.

Once the administration order has been made, the administrator is responsible for the affairs of the company. He has to prepare proposals to put before a meeting of the company's creditors which must be called as soon as practicable within three months of his appointment. The proposals must be aimed at achieving the one or more purposes for which the administration order was granted but, apart from that limitation, they can include whatever the administrator considers to be appropriate.

If the creditors' meeting rejects the administrator's proposals, the administrator must inform the court, which may either discharge the administration order or make such other orders as it considers appropriate. If the creditors' meeting approves the proposals, the administrator can proceed. Many administration orders are granted for purposes which include the sale of the business or part of the business as a going concern and, therefore, as far as buying a business from an administrator is concerned, the procedure is similar to an administrative receivership.

Corporate voluntary arrangements

This procedure was also introduced by the Insolvency Act 1986 and has been rarely used by itself. The directors, among others, may put forward a plan for a voluntary arrangement to an insolvency practitioner who, it is intended, will supervise the arrangement. The insolvency practitioner, or 'nominee', then has 28 days to formulate his proposals and to submit a report to the court recommending whether or not the proposals should be put to a meeting of the company's creditors. The creditors have the opportunity at the meeting to accept or reject the proposal. If accepted, the supervisor of the arrangement, as the insolvency practitioner is then known, can proceed with the proposal.

The problem with the procedure is that, in the 28 day period prior to the application to the court, the company has no protection from its creditors. As a consequence, it is likely that individual creditors may try to take any one of the various alternatives available to them in order to try to obtain an advantage over other creditors. The legal protection required for an insolvent company is perhaps best served by the use of the administration procedure in conjunction with the voluntary arrangement and, indeed, the approval of a voluntary arrangement is one of the purposes for which an administration order may be obtained.

The level of insolvencies

Administration orders and corporate voluntary arrangements appear to have had little impact on the levels of other forms of corporate insolvency. The following table shows the numbers of most of the different types of insolvency in the period since the introduction of the Insolvency Act 1986.

	1987	1988	1989	1990
Compulsory liquidations	4 116	3 667	4 020	5 977
Creditors' voluntary liquidations	7 323	5 760	6 436	8 974
Administration orders	21	47	43	58
Corporate voluntary arrangements	131	198	135	211

Source: DTI

In addition to the above, there were some 1 500 administrative receivership appointments during 1989 and this increased to nearly 4 000 in 1990. The trend appears to be increasing with over 1 500 appointments in the first three months of 1991.

Insolvency practitioners

All the insolvency appointments described above involve the appointment of an individual insolvency practitioner, or joint practitioners. One cannot appoint a firm of chartered accountants or other legal entity.

Since the implementation of the Insolvency Act 1986, any person who practises as an insolvency practitioner, and holds office in any of the procedures previously described, must be licensed. This applies to the office of liquidator, administrative receiver, administrator or supervisor of a voluntary arrangement. Licences to practise as an insolvency practitioner are granted by the Secretary of State for Trade and Industry or by any of the several professional bodies representing accountants, solicitors and insolvency practitioners which have been recognised by the Secretary of State for this purpose.

As at 31 December 1989 there were 1 778 insolvency practitioners who had been licensed by seven professional bodies, plus a small number of practitioners who had received their licences directly from the Secretary of State, with details as follows:

	No. of licences
Institute of Chartered Accountants in England and Wales	970
Insolvency Practitioners Association	263
Institute of Chartered Accountants in Scotland	205
Chartered Association of Certified Accountants	110
Institute of Chartered Accountants in Ireland	100
Law Society	97
Law Society of Scotland	33
	1 778
Direct authorization by Secretary of State	84
	1 862

Most insolvency practitioners are also qualified accountants with a small number of licences having been issued to members of the legal profession. A *Directory of Authorised Insolvency Practitioners*, giving full details of all current insolvency practitioners, is published by the Department of Trade and Industry and can be obtained from HMSO bookshops.

Prior to 1 April 1990, the granting of an insolvency licence depended on certain general levels of education, practical training and experience. Practitioners now have to pass specific insolvency examinations in order to apply for a licence.

They are also subject to various ethical guidelines issued by the DTI and the various recognised professional bodies. One of the principal requirements is that an insolvency practitioner must be seen to be completely independent, in connection with any insolvency appointment he takes. For example, any insolvency practitioner who has been an auditor, director or other office holder within a company, within the three years prior to the insolvency, or who has had a continuing professional relationship with a company within the same period, would be prevented from holding one of the insolvency appointments described above. The same restrictions apply to the firm in which an insolvency practitioner is a partner or to any member of such a firm.

Further protection is also given to creditors, in that any insolvency practitioner must have a general insurance bond for £250 000 as security for the proper performance of his duties. On each individual insolvency assignment, this general bond must be supplemented by a certificate of specific penalty for a value equivalent to the value of the assets for which he has responsibility.

It appears that the tightening up of these various controls has served to reduce the abuses which took place prior to the implementation of the Insolvency Act 1986. Insolvency practitioners have been described in the past as the guardians of the commercial morality of the country. If they show themselves to be unworthy of the trust placed in them by the creditors of an insolvent company, complaints may be made to the appropriate licensing authority or to the DTI and they may lose their licence.

Insolvency practitioners soon become well known in their local business community and this can lead to, perhaps unjustified, rumours about any companies whose premises they are seen entering. This was certainly true of the rumours which circulated about the Bank of England during the recession of the early 1970s when the late Sir Kenneth Cork, the chairman of the committee whose report led to the Insolvency Act 1986, was seen leaving the Bank in the early hours one morning.

Disqualification of directors

Since the implementation of the Insolvency Act 1986 and, more importantly, the Company Directors Disqualification Act 1986, the directors of limited companies can be disqualified for a period of time from acting as a director of a company or from taking part, either directly or indirectly, in the management of a company. These regulations apply not only to persons calling themselves directors or occupying the position of a director ('de facto' directors) but also to 'shadow' directors. A shadow director is defined as a person in accordance with whose instructions the directors of the company are accustomed to act. For example, if a person regularly attends board meetings and gives advice to the directors which they act upon, that person could be viewed as a shadow director and may be caught by the consequences of the legislation.

The grounds for which a director may be disqualified include the following:

- where a director is convicted of a criminal offence
- where a director is guilty of persistent breaches of companies legislation

- where a director is guilty of fraud, fraudulent trading or breach of duty in a winding up
- where a director is guilty of wrongful trading
- where a director is, or was, a director of a company which became insolvent and his conduct as a director makes him unfit to be concerned in the management of a company

Under the legislation, the official receiver (of a company in compulsory liquidation), or the liquidator (of a company in voluntary liquidation), or the administrator (of a company where an administration order is in force) or the administrative receiver (of a company in administrative receivership) is required to submit a return to the DTI on every person who was a director of the company in the three years prior to the relevant insolvency. If the insolvency practitioner considers that, in his opinion, a director or former director is unfit, then evidence of such unfitness should be included in the return.

The points on which the insolvency practitioner must base his judgement are detailed in the legislation. However, the following points have been considered to be most relevant in the large number of cases so far presented:

- carrying on trading when the director knew, or ought to have known, that the company was insolvent (wrongful trading)
- failing to keep proper books of account
- continuing to accept monies from customers in advance of the supply of goods when the company was in financial difficulties
- withholding large amounts of monies from the relevant authorities in respect of PAYE income tax, national insurance contributions or VAT
- drawing excessive levels of remuneration

After it has received the return from the insolvency practitioner, the DTI will decide whether or not to bring disqualification proceedings against the director concerned. The proceedings must be started within two years of the relevant insolvency. If the prosecution is successful, the director will be disqualified from being a director of a company, or from taking part in the management of a company, for a period of between two and fifteen years. This obviously has serious consequences for someone who is already a director of other companies. In the period since the introduction of the Insolvency Act 1986, the most common length of time for which directors have been disqualified is five years.

If the person who has been disqualified decides to defy the law and becomes a director of, or involved in the management of, another company without leave of the court and that company becomes insolvent, the person is personally liable for the debts of that second company. It is of course also a criminal offence. Furthermore, the personal liability may extend to any person who takes part in the management of the second company and acts on the instructions of a person who they know is disqualified.

The concept of personal liability also arises on the insolvent liquidation of a company. If a person was a director or shadow director in the 12 months before the liquidation, that person is prohibited for a period of five years from using the name of the company in liquidation in connection with any other company or business where they are either a director or concerned in the management of the company or business. This prohibition on the use of the name of an insolvent company also covers any trading name of a company or any name which suggests an association with the previous company. The legislation details certain circumstances where an otherwise prohibited name can be used and the permission of the court can also be obtained. If a director or shadow director contravenes the legislation, they will be committing a criminal offence and, again, they may find themselves being personally liable for the debts of the second company.

Fraudulent trading and wrongful trading

The Insolvency Act 1986 states that 'if in the course of the winding up of a company it appears that any business of the company has been carried on with intent to defraud creditors or creditors of any other person, or for any fraudulent purpose' the court may decide that anyone who was involved with the fraudulent trading may be required to make a contribution to the company's assets. The concept of fraudulent trading, and its consequences, have long been included in company legislation. Under the Insolvency Act 1986, fraudulent trading has now been supplemented by the concept of wrongful trading, with much wider implications for many directors of limited companies.

As in fraudulent trading, a successful action for wrongful trading will result in the director or shadow director having to make a contribution to the assets of the company in liquidation. Wrongful trading can only apply in an insolvent liquidation and the action is started by the liquidator. In order to be able to bring a successful action against a director or shadow director, the liquidator has to be able to prove that at some point in time prior to the liquidation of the company, the director knew, or ought to have known, that there was no reasonable prospect of the company avoiding going into insolvent liquidation. An action for wrongful trading will not be successful if the director is able to prove that he took every step to minimise the loss to the company's creditors.

The problem for directors is that, in assessing whether or not they took every step to minimise the loss to creditors, they are not only judged by their actual knowledge, skill and experience but by the knowledge, skill and experience that may reasonably be expected from a person who is carrying out the duties of the director whose ability is being questioned. The law is therefore attempting to lay down certain minimum acceptable standards on directors' behaviour. Once those minimum standards have been passed, the director will be judged on his actual standards.

The first reported example of wrongful trading was the case of Produce Marketing Consortium Limited. The company was incorporated in 1964 to act as an agent for the importing of fruit and, ever since 1981, there had been only two directors. At 30 September 1981, the company's balance sheet showed net assets of £2 518. In every year since 1981, the company had incurred trading losses.

In 1984, the bank granted an overdraft facility of £50 000 to the company which was secured by a debenture together with a personal guarantee from one of the directors. By this time, the company's liabilities exceeded its assets by some £58 000. The overdraft facility was subsequently increased to £75 000 with an increase in the director's personal guarantee to £50 000. By 1986 the company's situation had further deteriorated; the overdraft limit was often exceeded and cheques were being returned by the company's bankers. In January 1987, the company's auditors presented to the directors the draft accounts for each of the two years ended 30 September 1986. The accounts for the year ended 30 September 1985, which should have been filed at Companies' House by July 1986, showed a loss of some £56 000. Those for the following year showed a loss of approximately £30 000. In February 1987, the auditors wrote to the directors to confirm their earlier oral warnings that the directors could be liable for fraudulent trading.

In due course, the bank started to insist that the company's borrowings should be reduced and a total reduction of some £20 000 occurred in the period to September 1987, although amounts due to other creditors increased. The directors considered that they had no alternative but to continue trading in the period from February 1987 in order to protect certain perishable fruit belonging to the company which was held in cold store. In September 1987, the company went into creditors' voluntary liquidation and the liquidator brought an action for wrongful trading against the directors.

It was first necessary to prove a date from which there was no reasonable prospect that the company could avoid going into insolvent liquidation. Under company legislation, accounts for the year ended 30 September 1985 should have been delivered to the Registrar of Companies within ten months of that date, that is by 31 July 1986, and this was held to be the relevant date for the purpose of wrongful trading. Secondly, it was necessary to prove that the directors had not taken every step to minimise the potential loss to the company's creditors in the period since July 1986. Clearly this was not the case since they had continued to trade at a loss for over a year until the liquidation of the company and, even in the period since February 1987, the trading had not been limited to the protection of the fruit in cold store.

The liquidator had originally claimed over £107 000 from the directors. The judge considered that the amount that the directors should be liable to contribute was the amount by which the assets of the company had been depleted as a result of their actions. It was held that the two directors should be jointly and severally liable for £75 000.

Transactions at an undervalue

Where a company disposes of any of its property, for example, if a troubled company was to dispose of its business and assets prior to the onset of a formal insolvency, the sale could be attacked as a transaction at an undervalue by a subsequently appointed liquidator or administrator under the provisions of the Insolvency Act 1986.

Where the transaction takes place between a company and an unrelated third party, the subsequent formal insolvency may be at any time up to two years after the date of the transaction. If it is assumed that it is the sale of the business and assets of a company which is being scrutinised, the subsequently appointed liquidator or administrator will have to prove both that:

- the consideration actually paid for the business and assets was significantly less than they were actually worth
- at the time the transaction took place, the company was unable to pay its debts as and when they fell due or that the company became unable to pay its debts as a consequence of the transaction

Following a successful action, the court is given a wide discretion to make any order which it thinks fit for restoring the position to what it would have been if the company had not entered into the transaction in question. However, the court will not make an order if it is satisfied that the company which entered into the transaction did so in good faith, for the purpose of carrying on its business, and that, at the time it did so, there were reasonable grounds for believing that the transaction would benefit the company.

It should be obvious that these provisions in the legislation relating to transactions at an undervalue, can cause considerable difficulties for a purchaser contemplating the acquisition of the business and assets of a troubled company prior to any formal insolvency. Such a purchaser would not wish to proceed with the transaction, only to have it overturned by a subsequently appointed liquidator or administrator. Even if the purchaser was to win the legal action, the thought of a long, drawn out, legal battle is hardly to be cherished. If the sale was to proceed at a sufficiently high price such that there was no possibility that the transaction could subsequently be attacked, the deal may then not be economically viable for the purchaser.

The usual result of this dilemma for the potential purchaser is that, with yet another difficulty to overcome and with limited time available, the proposed purchase will be postponed until after the formal insolvency of the company.

Key point summary

- When considering the acquisition of a company in trouble prior to a formal insolvency, the potential purchaser should take good advice from a suitably qualified solicitor and accountant about possible insolvency offences.

4   Should I buy before or after an insolvency?

Buying a company in general

There are two ways of acquiring the business and assets of a company; either the whole of the share capital of the company can be acquired from the existing shareholders or the purchaser can acquire the business alone, usually together with some or all of the assets.

The purchase of a company by means of the acquisition of its share capital is usually straightforward and, in principal at least, a simple operation. As part of the completion process, the original owners of the share capital of the company will sign a share-transfer form and thus sell their shares to the new owners of the company. When the new owners have registered their shares, the transfer of the ownership is complete and little may have changed as far as both the general employees of the company are concerned and, indeed, the outside world, in the form of the company's customers and suppliers. The company is a separate legal entity and can carry on its business as usual; all that will have changed is the ownership of the company.

Of course in practice the actual transfer of the shares will be the culmination of a long period of negotiation between the sellers of the shares and the purchaser. At the same time the purchaser will conduct a detailed investigation into the affairs of the target company.

The company itself will not be a party to the eventual contract which will be between the original shareholders and the purchaser. The contract itself will be a weighty tome dealing with such matters as:

- who is selling what shares to whom
- the consideration to be paid for the shares

- how completion is to take place
- warranties given by the sellers
- undertakings to be given by the sellers
- future restrictions on the sellers
- the disclosure of information and various documents by the sellers

The consideration being paid for the share capital need not be payable in full on completion. In many cases, amounts are retained by the purchaser to set off against any breaches of the warranties given by the sellers. In addition, the final amount of the consideration payable for the share capital under the contract may only be determinable at some point in the future. For example, such determination may be made by reference to the performance of the company – its profitability – in the intervening period.

Probably the most important, and certainly the most discussed, section of the contract will be that dealing with the various warranties given by the original shareholders to the purchaser of those shares. The original shareholders will have to state that all the warranties which they are giving are accurate and true and the many pages of the warranties themselves will cover such topics as:

- the accounts and management accounts of the company up to the date of sale
- the solvency of the company
- all the directors and employees of the company and any related pension schemes
- the ownership and condition of the company's fixed assets, particularly its properties
- all contracts and agreements entered into by the company
- the general business of the company
- the taxation affairs of the company
- any statements made or documents supplied by the sellers to the purchaser

The second method of buying a healthy company is where a purchaser acquires only the business of the target company, as a going concern, and takes over the employees' contracts of employment. The acquisition will also cover some, if not all, of the fixed and chattel assets of the company. Such a purchase can also deal with the acquisition of a division or other part of a larger company.

In this case, the parties to the contract will be the target company itself which is selling the business and assets, and the purchaser of those assets. The original shareholders will retain ownership of the shares in the target company.

Under the contract, the purchaser will usually acquire the following assets:

- any contracts in progress
- work in progress and stock
- relevant freehold and leasehold properties and other fixed assets
- goodwill, including the name or trading name of the company
- the employees

In such acquisitions, it is normal for all the liabilities of the target company, up to the date of completion, to remain as liabilities of the target company, with the exception of those liabilities which the purchaser may wish to take over, such as hire purchase or leasing liabilities attaching to any assets which are being acquired.

It rarely makes any sense for the company's cash in hand or cash at bank to be sold as part of the assets of the company and, similarly, it is usual for the debtors to remain the responsibility of the target company, thus obviating the necessity of valuing, and providing warranties for, such debtors. However, it is often the case that, after completion, the purchaser will take over the collection of debtors as agent for the target company, in order to minimise any disruption to the customers of the business. The realisations from such debtor collections would usually be paid in to a separate bank account and then remitted to the original company at regular intervals.

Since it is only the assets and business which are being acquired, the contract between the parties is usually very much simpler than is the case with a purchase of shares. In particular, the warranties given by the vendor are usually considerably reduced in a business sale agreement because all the liabilities remain with the original company with the exception of, in general, those liabilities which the purchaser expressly wishes to take over.

Where a sale of the business and assets has taken place and the sale is not of a division or other part of a larger company, the vendor company will often proceed into members' voluntary liquidation. The remaining debts are collected and all of the company's liabilities are paid, and the residual funds in the company are then distributed to the shareholders.

Buying a company in trouble prior to insolvency

Purchasing the shares of a company in trouble before it has entered into a formal insolvency, can be fraught with difficulties and complications.

Perhaps the purchaser started the investigation process assuming that he was buying a healthy company, only to find out during the investigation process that the company is in serious financial trouble. Perhaps he has purposely targeted a known company in trouble in the hope that it can be acquired cheaply. Whatever the reason, once the purchaser discovers that he is investigating a troubled company, his principal difficulty is likely to be a shortage of time.

The purchaser must undertake a very thorough and detailed investigation in order to ascertain the price to be paid for the company, both in terms of the required purchase consideration and in terms of the amount he will have to spend in order to restore the company to solvency.

This 'additional' consideration is an important point to bear in mind by the purchaser and one that can easily be overlooked in the expectation that a bargain is being acquired. Most purchasers will give at least some consideration to the earnings capability of the company, compared with the price that is being paid for the company; the return on capital employed. It is all too easy to overlook the additional capital required by the company immediately after the acquisition and the diluting effect this may have on the calculation of the return on capital employed. The purchaser of the shares of the troubled company will therefore have to spend a far greater part of his investigation in reviewing, or even preparing, the various forecasts for the post-acquisition period in order to calculate the amount of this extra consideration.

Unforeseen problems . . .

A group of companies sold its two manufacturing subsidiaries, in a small management buy-out, to the directors of the subsidiaries for £40 000. The group had been going through a difficult trading period because of the recession and had been forced to take extended credit from its suppliers. The creditors of individual companies within the group were not worried because the group as a whole was financially sound. As soon as the sale took place, however, the creditors of the two subsidiaries insisted on a return to normal credit terms because they had lost the financial backing of the other group companies. The new directors of the subsidiaries had to find an additional £150 000 within the space of some three months and they did not succeed. The companies went into receivership some six months after the sale took place.

The purchaser will also have to spend a considerable amount of time in determining the causes of the company's difficulties. If the shares of the company in trouble are being acquired, the purchaser will inherit the causes of the company's difficulties immediately and he must be certain that he is aware of these problems so that they can be eliminated as soon as possible.

During the investigation, the purchaser may discover that the causes of the company's difficulties are too fundamental and that recovery is impossible, for example if the company is solely involved in a dying industry with no prospect of diversification. In such a case, the purchaser should not hesitate to withdraw from the negotiations as soon as possible. It must be stressed that we are not talking about a simple turnaround situation but a turnaround with the added factor that the company is legally insolvent; it cannot pay its debts as and when they fall due and, in the extreme case, its liabilities exceed its assets.

Where the troubled company has a shortfall of assets when compared with liabilities, it is likely also to be unable to pay its debts as and when they fall due and the payment of just £1 for the share capital could be an expensive price to pay. After the acquisition, the purchaser will have to pay off the liabilities of the company, inject further funds in the form of working capital, and risk the possibility of wrongful, or even fraudulent, trading if the acquisition does not succeed.

There may be instances where the purchase of the shares of a company in trouble, outside a formal insolvency, could be justified, for example, if the purchaser can provide sufficient additional turnover almost immediately in order to stem the company's losses straight away and restore it to profitability. Such a purchase may also be considered where a company is facing the loss of a key customer or supplier because of an impending insolvency. Provided the costs of restoring the proposed acquisition to solvency are less than the costs of replacing that customer or supplier, then the acquisition may be justified.

The problem is that the potential purchaser rarely has the time available to carry out the depth of investigation required in such a case. He needs to establish the full potential cost of the acquisition, the extent of all of the liabilities of the company, including contingent liabilities, the amount of additional working capital which is required and so on. At the same time, the pressure from creditors, in particular the company's bank, will probably be increasing and the existing shareholders are likely to be doing everything in their power to extricate themselves with all haste from all of the problems, and all of the potential personal liabilities, with which they are faced.

In such a case, the usual warranties which are included in an agreement for the sale of shares may not be especially useful, particularly if the maximum liability for any breaches of warranty is limited to the price paid for the shares, which may have been minimal.

Of course, the alternative course of action in this situation is to consider the acquisition of only the business and assets of the company in trouble but, again, such a route can often be fraught with difficulties for both the purchaser and the seller.

The principal difficulties for the purchaser will, similarly, be those arising from a shortage of time. Which are the profitable contracts? What employees are necessary for the, perhaps, slimmed down business? Is it necessary to acquire all of the assets of the target company? Will a fair and reasonable price be paid for the assets and, if not, what is the possibility of a court setting the transaction aside as a sale at an undervalue? All these questions will need to be answered at a time when the inevitable pressure from the company's creditors is increasing.

The problems for the seller, or the directors of the target company, may stem from slightly different considerations. It is likely that the directors of the target company will be dealing with only one prospective purchaser and, because of the financial trouble which the company is facing, it is probable that the price under discussion for the business and assets of the company will not be sufficient to discharge all of the liabilities of the company. No matter how fair and reasonable the price, without the injection of further, additional funds, the company will inevitably face insolvent liquidation.

Welfab Engineers Limited

The company began to run into financial difficulties during 1982, and the directors instructed agents to place the company's factory on the market discreetly. At the same time, the directors were negotiating the sale of the company's business and assets with other third parties.

After several abortive discussions with various third parties for the sale of either the factory or the business, the directors concluded a deal whereby the business and assets of the company were sold to another company, together with all of the employees, including the directors. Although the sale price secured both the continuation of the company's business and the continued employment of all of the workforce, the price paid was less than the agents' previous valuation of the factory alone and less than a previous offer which had been received for the factory and subsequently rejected by the directors. The proceeds of the sale were also insufficient to discharge all of the company's liabilities and the company went into liquidation.

The liquidator commenced an action against the directors of the original company for breach of duty which was eventually dismissed by the judge. However, it is important to note that the company went into liquidation prior to the implementation of the Insolvency Act 1986. If that Act had been in force at the time of the liquidation, it is considered that the directors may have found themselves accused of wrongful trading in that they may not have taken all the steps necessary to minimise the loss to the company's creditors.

So although a purchaser may have very sound reasons initially for acquiring a particular company, if the preliminary enquiries and investigations reveal severe financial problems, in other words that it is a company in trouble, it would be better to defer the purchase until after a formal insolvency of the company has taken place.

Buying a company in trouble after insolvency

The acquisition of a company in trouble is most likely to fall into this category. The potential purchaser has either thought better about proceeding with a pre-insolvency acquisition and approached the insolvency practitioner after the formal insolvency or he has become aware of the potential purchase after the insolvency.

In Chapter 3 we discussed the various formal insolvency procedures. The business and assets of an insolvent company could be acquired from:

- an administrative receivership
- an administration
- a creditors' voluntary liquidation
- a corporate voluntary arrangement

It is most likely that a business will be purchased as a going concern (the business *and* assets of the company) from an administrative receiver and the rest of this book will make this assumption when discussing the purchase of an insolvent business. Any differences in dealing either with an administrator or a liquidator will be highlighted. Moreover, and in line with common parlance, the adjective 'administrative' will be dropped. It is stressed that the resultant 'receiver' should not be confused with the other appointments of receivers which can be found, for example under the Law of Property Act 1925.

It is worth stressing that the sale of the shares of a company, prior to a formal insolvency, is a true 'going concern' sale. After a formal insolvency, the term 'going concern' sale invariably means the sale of certain, or all, of the company's assets together with the business but without any of the associated liabilities.

When a receiver sells a business as a going concern, certain of the company's previous problems will automatically have been eliminated. As it is only the business and assets which are being acquired, the problems of insolvency are removed, provided the purchaser does not pay too much for the business and assets. No creditors will be acquired, unless the purchaser wishes to take over any liabilities such as hire purchase or leasing liabilities or guarantee obligations. In theory, the purchaser will be presented with a relatively clean business which can start trading as soon as the contract is completed. However, this does not mean that the purchaser will avoid problems completely. A sale of a business, let alone an insolvent business, is rarely a matter which is completed with a clean break. There will inevitably be work or contracts in progress which the receiver will wish to hand over to the purchaser. Cash flow is likely to be a problem during the initial period of trading, until the new company's debtors pay up.

The purchaser has already been advised that he should regard the purchase of a business from a receiver as the purchase of a collection of assets. However, it is not simply an asset purchase because at least certain elements of the previous business will also be acquired. It is therefore important that the purchaser's investigation of the insolvent company is thorough. He needs to be able to identify the causes of failure of the old company and so reduce the chances of carrying them over to the new company. Although poor management is the most common cause of failure, the purchaser should not assume that, if the management is not taken over into the new company, no problems will be transferred. Similarly, if there was a complete lack of financial control in the insolvent company, it may not be sufficient simply to put adequate control procedures in place.

The purchaser must try and conduct an adequate investigation into the insolvent company, notwithstanding the severe time constraints being placed on him by the receiver. Those constraints may be eased somewhat if the purchaser uses a suitably qualified team to undertake the investigation. The composition of such a team is discussed in the next chapter.

Key point summary

- Prior to a formal insolvency it is imperative that a potential purchaser carries out a detailed investigation, but time constraints may prevent this.
- If a detailed investigation cannot be carried out, do not proceed.
- The purchaser must ensure that he is aware of any 'hidden' post-acquisition costs which are likely to arise.
- The purchaser should give very serious thought to waiting until after a formal insolvency; the price will be cheaper and fewer problems inherited.
- Even when buying a business as a going concern after an insolvency, the causes of the insolvency should never be ignored.

5 Who should advise me?

Once the target company has been identified, the purchaser and his acquisition team should be ready to start an investigation. The team may consist of a number of people drawn from the purchaser's existing business and from his external advisors. The size and composition of the acquisition team will depend largely on the size and status of the target company.

If the purchaser is buying a troubled company prior to a formal insolvency, the formal insolvency may not be far away. For this reason, and because the purchaser will wish to pre-empt a competitive bid, he will have to act quickly. Similarly, if the purchaser is buying a business as a going concern from an insolvency practitioner, he will also be subject to time constraints imposed this time by the administrative receiver or administrator of the company. If the purchaser cannot meet the timetable set by the insolvency practitioner, other purchasers may be able to do so and he will miss his chance. The purchaser should therefore think about his acquisition team at an early stage, when the decision is first made to embark on an acquisition strategy.

Depending upon the size and nature of the particular acquisition, the acquisition team may consist of a mixture of:

- an 'in-house' team
- the purchaser's auditors or accountants
- specialist insolvency accountants
- solicitors
- property agents or valuers
- other advisors as required

In general terms, the purchaser should be using both internal and external advisors who are used to working outside normal working hours. Buying a company in trouble, especially from an insolvency practitioner, is not a nine-to-five job; time is critical and decisions often have to be made immediately. It can be very frustrating, to say the least, for the purchaser to telephone his accountants or solicitors at 5.05 p.m. to enquire about the effects of a clause which has just been inserted into the contract due to be signed tomorrow, only to find that the switchboard closed down five minutes earlier.

The negotiations over the sale contract can often continue until the early hours of the morning, or even overnight, because the solicitors acting for the insolvency practitioner will probably have been instructed to continue until the contract has been agreed. If the purchaser's advisors insist on leaving at 5.00 p.m., there could well be an alternative purchaser who is waiting in the next room.

The purchaser should be aware that the principal function of his external advisors is to ensure that he is fully and adequately informed about all the areas of the acquisition which the purchaser cannot staff from within his own company. Their engagement will not necessarily guarantee that the acquisition will proceed.

In order to ascertain the composition of a minimum team, the purchaser must ensure that he has covered the following basic areas of experience:

- technical
- accountancy
- legal
- insolvency
- negotiation skills

In-house team

The in-house team, which is drawn from the purchaser's existing business or company, is one of the most important ingredients of the total acquisition team. Dependent upon both the size of the existing operation and the size of the acquisition, the team may vary from the managing director or finance director alone, to a permanent, specialist team which is called together whenever an acquisition is being considered.

The principal objectives of the in-house team are, firstly, to assess the fit of the proposed acquisition against the previously defined target profile and against the existing business of the purchaser and, secondly, to assess the intangible benefits of the acquisition; those benefits which cannot easily be expressed in financial terms. The team will also be in a strong position to evaluate the management strength of the target company.

The team should include a senior accountant, such as the financial director, and if the purchaser does not employ one, more reliance will have to be placed on external advice, from the purchaser's auditors or accountants, for example. If the purchaser is in the same business as that of the target company, the team should also include a technical specialist who is conversant with the target's business. If the purchaser is diversifying into a new area of business, he should seriously consider taking on a specialist who can advise on the technical side of the acquisition.

The purchaser should also consider including the person who will be in charge of the acquisition after the purchase has been completed, assuming that the target company's directors will not be left solely in charge. This person is going to be critical to the success or failure of the acquisition and the period of investigation is an ideal time for him to get to know the target company. His first management task will be to ensure that the acquisition team works as a whole and performs speedily and efficiently. He should also be responsible for compiling the investigation report.

We have already discussed some of the pitfalls of buying a company in trouble and it is to be hoped that any potential purchaser has begun to appreciate some of the inherent risks involved. Consequently, the purchaser should also be able to appreciate that it could be a false economy to use the wrong advisors and it may prove to be a very costly mistake. It is very easy for the purchaser to think that he can make do with internal advisors, for reasons of cost alone, when they are not sufficiently qualified. He must use the right people for the job.

After the investigation has been completed, the purchaser will have to decide on the individual who is going to conduct the negotiation. This may be the purchaser himself or a member of his internal team, or the responsibility may be delegated to one of the external advisors. The purchaser should bear the following points in mind:

- The negotiator should be impartial. If emotions are allowed to come into play, too high a price may be paid or a good deal may be lost.
- The negotiations should be conducted by only one individual on behalf of the purchaser. A solicitor will then assist in negotiating the detailed terms of the contract. If more than one person takes part, it is possible that different terms will be agreed. It is also very frustrating for the vendor if he does not know precisely who he is supposed to be dealing with.
- Negotiation is an art. If the purchaser does not consider that he has the necessary skills, he should ensure that the negotiations are carried out by someone who has. This will be particularly relevant where it is the purchaser's first attempt at an acquisition. If the purchase is being negotiated with an insolvency practitioner, it should be remembered that he will be both a seasoned negotiator and completely impartial. It is also likely that he will be an exceptionally good poker player!

External auditors of the purchaser

The potential role of the purchaser's external auditors or accountants varies. Even if the purchaser has adequate in-house financial expertise, it is likely that the external accountants will be required to advise on such matters as:

- the apportionment of the total purchase consideration between, for example, property, other fixed assets, goodwill and so on
- the availability of tax losses within the proposed target company
- whether to make the purchase through a subsidiary (existing or newly formed) or directly

- whether the acquisition would present an opportunity for the purchaser to become incorporated if he is not already
- general taxation advice

In certain circumstances, it may also be appropriate for the purchaser's auditors or accountants to conduct the detailed investigation on behalf of the purchaser although it is preferable for such accountants to be well versed in the subject of insolvency. If they do not have this experience, the investigation may take too long and time is not on the purchaser's side. Moreover, as accountants charge by the hour, a lengthy investigation will be more expensive, which is not to say that any corners should be cut. Accountants who are only trained as auditors may be trying to carry out an audit on the target company and that is not what is required. The purchaser may not have enough experience to give precise instructions to the accountants so he must ensure that, if external accountants are required for the detailed investigation, they should be able both to make commercial decisions and to focus on the important issues.

With this in mind, the purchaser should meet with the partner concerned both to agree the fee for the investigation and to have discussions about the people who are actually going to carry out the investigation. Ideally, the purchaser should meet the team and ascertain for himself that they are not too junior and that they have conducted such investigations before. This is not being pedantic; there is too much at stake for the purchaser to risk any mistakes.

Specialist insolvency accountants

The purchaser's auditors or accountants may have a department which specialises in insolvency matters. In this case, it will be a simple matter to seek expert advice from such a department. Otherwise, and particularly where the purchaser's legal advisors are not well acquainted with insolvency law, the purchaser should seriously consider enrolling an insolvency specialist on the acquisition team.

The role of an insolvency specialist could vary from simply giving advice on a report which has already been prepared by other members of the acquisition team through to the investigation itself. In particular, the insolvency specialist will be able to advise on:

- whether or not an offer should be made for a business prior to any formal insolvency
- an assessment of the risks involved if a pre-insolvency acquisition of shares is being considered
- the likely effect of the insolvency or pending insolvency on the ongoing business of the target company
- any potential liabilities in respect of employees
- potential problems facing the directors of the target company (particularly relevant where the purchaser is thinking of reemploying such directors)
- the quality and ability of the management of the target company
- the likely net worth of the business

The points already discussed, referring to the purchaser's accountants or auditors, apply equally to specialist insolvency accountants; the level of work should be defined, a fee should be agreed and, if an investigation is being carried out, the composition and quality of the team should be discussed. Insolvency practitioners have varying degrees of experience and it may not be a wise decision to use for an investigation, an insolvency practitioner whose only practical experience has been confined to small liquidations and personal bankruptcy.

Insolvency specialists are used to undertaking investigations at short notice on behalf of banks and other lending institutions and will be able to work quickly. Where the purchaser is considering the acquisition of a business as a going concern from an insolvency practitioner, an insolvency specialist will obviously have a useful understanding of the way in which other practitioners work and think.

This advantage could be maximised if the purchaser took on an insolvency specialist who had had previous dealings with the insolvency practitioner who was conducting the sale. Furthermore, if the purchaser was planning to buy from a receiver or administrator, it would be sensible to use an insolvency accountant who had experience of receiverships and administrations.

If the purchase involves a troubled company prior to a formal insolvency, an experienced insolvency accountant could give the purchaser a positive advantage because of his negotiating experience.

Solicitors

Solicitors need to advise the purchaser on all legal matters connected with the acquisition and, in particular, agreeing the sale contract which will have been prepared by the solicitors acting for the insolvency practitioner.

It has already been said that, if a company in trouble is being acquired, the purchaser's solicitors should be experienced in insolvency law. There are two reasons; firstly, the solicitors will be able to give sound advice on the particular problems which may arise in insolvent, or potentially insolvent, cases thus reducing the amount of work required from any insolvency specialists from the accounting profession. Secondly, the solicitor with insolvency experience is more likely to appreciate the reasons behind the various clauses in the sale agreement and the commercial decisions which often have to be taken during the course of such acquisitions. They will also be aware of the speed with which such transactions inevitably have to take place.

If the purchaser does not have his own solicitors, he could approach the insolvency practitioner from whom he hopes to buy the business or any other, preferably local, insolvency practitioner for advice. The insolvency practitioner will usually be able to recommend a short list of solicitors with appropriate insolvency experience.

Property agents or valuers

If the proposed acquisition involves the purchase of any significant freehold or leasehold property, the purchaser should engage the services of appropriate agents. At the very least, such agents will be able to value the properties under consideration. Unless peculiar circumstances exist, full, structural surveys of the properties are not usually required, although the agents' advice should be sought on this question. The agents will also be able to advise on alternative uses for the target company's properties, any potential planning problems, and so forth.

Other advisors

Other advisors who may be required in certain circumstances will include:

- stock takers or valuers
- patent or trade mark agents
- actuaries with regard to any pension schemes
- plant and machinery specialists

Bankers

The purchaser may retain a team of merchant bankers, who amongst other things, may advise on acquisitions. However, the inclusion of bankers in a chapter on advisors is to remind purchasers that early discussions should be held with the purchaser's bankers, or other lenders, if the purchaser needs to borrow money to fund the acquisition.

From the seller's point of view, there is nothing more frustrating than to have otherwise successful negotiations grind to a halt because the purchaser is unable to raise the capital required to complete the purchase. From the purchaser's perspective, there are few things more financially embarrassing than to find out, perhaps after a substantial deposit has been paid, that further funds are not available.

The pitfalls

It cannot be stressed too much, particularly when buying a company in trouble, that the purchaser should seek proper and adequate advice on all aspects of the proposed acquisition. The purchaser must seek to minimise the risks involved. Where outside advisors are used, the purchaser should give them clear and definitive instructions in writing at all times.

If adequate advice is not obtained, the purchaser can face considerable loss of time and expense, including the possible failure of the acquired business. Such a failure may also damage the financial health of the purchaser's original business. The following case histories illustrate this point.

(a) **Company A** purchased the business and assets of a food processing company from the administrative receivers. No accountancy advice was taken and too high a price was paid for the assets and business, the business did not succeed and, within 12 months, Company A itself went into receivership. The directors of Company A were caught by personal guarantees to Company A's bankers.

(b) **Company B** purchased the business and assets of a building company from the administrative receivers. The purchaser's solicitors did not have insolvency experience and the contract made no reference to employees. Following an industrial tribunal, Company B was held to be responsible for the liabilities of all of the employees of the previous company who had been dismissed by the receivers immediately prior to the sale.

(c) **Company C** sold its chain of hotels as a going concern immediately prior to a creditors' voluntary liquidation of the company. Although the sale contract made reference to the liability (upon Company C) for the payroll for all the staff for the month terminating on the date of completion, it did not make adequate reference as to how such liability would be discharged. The purchaser subsequently had to fund an additional month's payroll in order to retain all the staff at a time when his cash resources were already stretched. There were insufficient assets left in the liquidation of Company C, after the payment of secured creditors, for the purchaser to obtain any more than a nominal dividend in respect of his unsecured claim.

Key point summary

- The purchaser should identify his acquisition team at an early stage.
- Ideally the team should include the individual who is going to manage the target company after the acquisition.
- The team must include people with adequate knowledge of insolvency.
- The team must be able to act quickly and efficiently.

6 Should I do an investigation?

All potential purchasers run an investigation before buying any item. Either knowingly or unknowingly, the purchaser will identify the reason for making the purchase, ensure that the proposed purchase meets that aim and finally, will check that the price is right. The depth of investigation will depend upon what is being acquired, the buyer's knowledge of the proposed purchase and how much is being spent.

The purchase of a company, and particularly the purchase of a company in trouble, must start with a detailed investigation. This chapter sets the scene for the investigation and the next chapter gives the purchaser a framework in which to conduct it; to ensure that the proposed purchase will do what he intends and to ensure he pays a reasonable price.

The main objectives of an investigation are:

- to get to know the company
- to try to establish the causes of the company's difficulty
- to identify potential problem areas
- to provide the basis for a valuation of the company

Most of the above will fall out naturally during the course of the investigation but trying to establish the causes of the company's difficulties will probably call for a certain amount of detective work. The company's statutory accounts are likely to be out of date and if management accounts exist, their quality must be questionable. If the directors of the company are asked for their opinion on the reasons for the difficulties, their response must at least be doubted. After all, it was the directors who caused the company to get into trouble and they are likely to blame everyone and everything but themselves. They could even be planning to talk the purchaser into giving them positions with the new company after it has been acquired.

Following an insolvency of the company, the management may be planning to buy back the business and assets from the insolvency practitioner and the purchaser could find that he is talking to a potential competitor. In an extreme case the management and other employees may refuse to talk to, or be employed by, any other purchaser because such a buy-back is being planned. In one case this meant that the receiver was unable to negotiate the sale of a good, profitable business to anyone but the existing management. Unfortunately, because they were under-capitalised from the outset, the business failed again within a few months of the acquisition.

The company's management will be far more willing to talk to a purchaser if the outcome of the sale affects them financially; they may have a potential liability under personal guarantees to the company's bank or in respect of a leasehold property, and they will usually have guaranteed some of the company's hire purchase or leasing agreements. They will want to ensure that the sale achieves the highest possible price, or perhaps includes a particular leased asset that is surplus to the company's requirements. The purchaser is certainly not likely to hear the truth about the company's difficulties.

If the purchaser is buying from an insolvency practitioner, he must remember that the insolvency practitioner will only have been involved with the company for a comparatively short period of time. He may not have investigated the affairs of the company before his appointment and even if he had, the time involved would have been limited and he may not have been asked to investigate the reasons behind the company's failure. After all, the main purpose behind the appointment of the insolvency practitioner is to realise the best price for the business and assets of the company, for the benefit of the company's creditors.

Any purchaser wanting to investigate the affairs of a target company also faces a major problem of confidentiality. If for example, the target was an advertising company where the value of the company lay in the knowledge of the employees and its customer database, it is highly unlikely that a potential purchaser of the business will be allowed to have access to either until negotiations are at a very advanced stage.

What investigation is required?

The depth of the investigation required by a prospective purchaser will depend upon the assets or business which are being acquired. In an insolvency, the simplest purchase will probably involve only the chattel assets of the company, such as plant and machinery and stock, in which case the investigation will be minimal. It will probably be limited to checking the extent and ownership of the assets. The degree of investigation work required will increase if other assets, such as freehold or leasehold properties, are being purchased.

In virtually all cases where a purchaser acquires a business as a going concern from an insolvency practitioner, he is still acquiring only the assets and the business and this will serve to limit the degree of investigation work. Although a purchaser should not be concerned with, for example, the quantum of the unsecured liabilities of the company, he may still want to find out who the principal suppliers are in order to ensure continuity of supply.

There is also the case where a purchaser is considering the acquisition of the shares of a company in trouble prior to any insolvency. In this case, the investigation procedures must be both detailed and thorough. The purchaser needs to become as knowledgeable as possible about all aspects of the target company and collect sufficient information to enable him to place a value on the company. This will then enable the purchaser to make an offer to the shareholders for their shares in the company.

The purchaser is seeking both qualitative and quantitative information. He wants to find out about such things as the quality of the company's management and the reasons for the company's difficulties and he needs to quantify the value of the company's assets and liabilities, bearing in mind that the accounts will probably be very much out of date and management accounts or other management information may well be non-existent.

In any troubled company which has not yet entered into a formal insolvency, time may well be critical as the arrival of the bailiffs or a winding-up petition may be imminent. Thus the amount of time available for the investigation is likely to be limited.

Even if a business is being acquired from an insolvency practitioner, time is still likely to be of the essence; there will probably be other interested parties and the receiver or administrator may have set an early deadline for the sale of the business or may be about to dismiss staff whom the purchaser wishes to interview or re-employ after the purchase.

The rest of this chapter will assume that the potential purchaser is trying to buy a company in trouble from its shareholders, where the company has not entered into a formal insolvency; thus, a full and detailed investigation is required. If the purchaser is buying the business or assets of a company from an insolvency practitioner, the investigation can be reduced and the purchaser should tailor both the rest of this chapter and the next chapter accordingly.

The investigation timetable

In an ideal world, the prospective purchaser would take the whole of the acquisition team to the target company. The investigation would then take place during the course of one, perhaps lengthy, visit. A complete investigation report would be prepared at the conclusion of the visit and an offer would then be made.

Unfortunately, the investigation process is likely to be far more time consuming and require far more in the way of 'management' by the purchaser than is first realised. Furthermore, if a pre-insolvency investigation is being undertaken, it is likely that the investigation will have to be carried out with a certain degree of discretion on the part of the investigation team.

The investigation should begin with a review of the information held in the company's file at Companies House, together with any available sales or product literature. If the purchaser is buying the business and assets of an insolvent company, he should also have received a copy of the sales particulars from the insolvency practitioner. This may include more current accounting information than is available from Companies House and a certain amount of detailed information about the assets which are being sold.

The rest of the investigation process will probably fall into four distinct phases:

- an initial visit by the purchaser's senior management to obtain their first impressions of the proposed acquisition, if these are not already known, to set the scene for the rest of the investigation and to determine the basic terms of reference
- the detailed investigation proper where the bulk of the required information is obtained
- the collection of further necessary reports, such as property valuations, from third parties
- a follow-up visit to obtain any sensitive information and to discuss fully any problem areas which have come to light as a result of information obtained in the earlier phases of the investigation

The final aspect of the investigation process is the compilation of a written report. This is an important part of the investigation and should not be overlooked. It serves to crystallize the thoughts of the investigation team and should set down the various strengths and weaknesses of the acquisition.

The statement of estimated financial position (or statement of affairs)

When an insolvency practitioner investigates the affairs of a company, one of the most important documents prepared is a statement of the estimated financial position of the company as at a specific point in time. This statement is also known as a statement of affairs. The statement is usually prepared as at the latest convenient point in time, such as the last month end so that, hopefully, up to date lists of debtors and creditors will be available. An example of such a statement of estimated financial position is given in Appendix 2 (see page 129). A similar statement should be prepared by the purchaser of a company in trouble.

The statement of affairs has two important functions; firstly, it summarises all the assets and liabilities of the company and, therefore, ultimately shows the net worth of the company. Secondly, by comparing the net worth of the company at whatever point in time is chosen with the net worth of the company at the date of the last audited accounts, one can deduce the likely profit or loss that the company has made in the period since the last accounts were prepared. In order to facilitate this comparison, the statement of affairs usually includes a restatement of the company's last accounts. From this it is easy to compare the totals of the various individual categories of assets and liabilities between periods, both to ensure completeness and to provide scope for further questions to be asked, for example, where significant differences in value are noted at the two respective dates.

The estimated values of the assets which are included in the statement of affairs are usually stated on the bases of an estimate of their going concern value and an estimate of their underlying security or forced sale value.

The going concern values, as the term implies, attempt to value the assets of the company on a true, going concern basis, on the assumption that the business is continued in more or less its current form.

If one starts with the 'book' values for the assets concerned, certain adjustments may have to be made in order to arrive at their going concern values. For example:

- the freehold or leasehold properties may have to be written up, or down, in order to arrive at the current market value
- plant and machinery may have been overdepreciated
- computers and other pieces of highly technological equipment will almost certainly have been underdepreciated
- stock may have to be written down to take account of excessive, old or redundant items
- debtors may have to be written down to take account of uncollectable accounts
- intangible assets may have been excluded from the company's balance sheet in the past but have a significant value to the prospective purchaser

In broad terms, the purchaser is trying to establish a value for the assets of the company which would equate to a purchase of those assets in their current condition and for their current use. If time permits and if the value of the assets is significant, it may be necessary to obtain a valuation of the assets from a professional valuer. This will almost certainly be required in order to arrive at a current value for any freehold or leasehold properties. However, for most of the chattel assets and stock, the purchaser will probably have to rely on his own experience and judgement together with general advice from his professional advisors.

The second basis of valuation which is usually incorporated into the statement of affairs is the underlying security or forced sale value. On this basis, the assumption is that the assets do not form part of a going concern business and that they are to be disposed of, for example, by way of auction in a relatively short period of time. In other words, if the business failed completely, this is the remaining value which could reasonably be expected to be realised from the assets concerned. In most cases, the forced sale value of a particular asset or category of asset would show a considerable reduction on the going concern value. For example, debtors arising out of a contractual relationship, where the realisation of the debtors depends on the continued performance by the company under the contract, may well be completely irrecoverable in a forced sale situation and, indeed, the cessation of the contract by the company in such circumstances will probably lead to claims against the company for breach of contract or other damages.

Furthermore, it may be appropriate to include as creditors in a forced sale, other claims from creditors which would only arise in such circumstances. These may include:

- employees' claims for lieu of notice and redundancy monies
- repayments of grants received by the company

- residual claims from hire purchase or leasing companies
- dilapidation claims from landlords

The statement of affairs will therefore be seen to be an attempt to establish the net worth of the company in both 'best' and 'worst' scenarios. It is also worth noting that the statement of affairs is set out in a format which will not be familiar to most businessmen and many of their professional advisors. The format is dictated by the provisions of the insolvency legislation and shows where the respective classes of creditor rank in terms of the distribution of assets.

The assets on the statement are principally divided into the two classifications; fixed and floating charge assets. In the example shown in Appendix 2, the principal lender to the company is a bank which has been granted a debenture secured by a fixed and floating charge over the assets of the company as security for the company's borrowings. The fixed charge assets are those assets which are covered by the bank's fixed charge and where the bank is first entitled to the proceeds of sale. The situation is analogous to a building society mortgage on a residential property and, indeed, the principal fixed charge assets are usually property, both freehold and leasehold, together with debtors and investments. In practice the purchaser may find that there are several creditors with fixed charges. Their priority will be determined either by arrangement between the fixed charge creditors or by the dates on which the charges were granted, with the earliest charge having the first priority.

The floating charge assets are all those remaining assets of the company which are not covered by the fixed charge. The sale proceeds obtained from these assets will be distributed to meet the remaining claims of creditors in the following order of priority:

(a) preferential creditors, such as the Inland Revenue in respect of PAYE income tax, the Department of Social Security in respect of National Insurance contributions, Customs and Excise in respect of VAT and the employees of the company in respect of arrears of pay and holiday pay
(b) any debenture holder to the extent that it has not been repaid under its fixed charge
(c) unsecured creditors such as trade suppliers, employees' claims in respect of payments in lieu of notice and redundancy payments, residual claims in respect of finance obligations (lease and hire purchase agreements), directors' loans
(d) shareholders

Within each classification of creditor, the claims of individual creditors rank equally among each other.

The preparation of a statement of affairs will also have a further benefit for a purchaser who needs to borrow money to help fund the purchase. A bank will usually only be willing to advance funds based upon the value of the available security. Normally this will be based upon a percentage of the forced sale value of the fixed charge assets and so the preparation of a statement of affairs will enable the purchaser to gauge the likely value of the available security. He should not assume that another bank would be willing simply to take over the company's existing banking facilities; the statement of affairs is likely to show that the existing bank is undersecured.

When only the business and assets are being acquired after a formal insolvency, the preparation of a statement of affairs will still be a useful exercise for the purchaser, although he need not be especially particular about the total amount of the claims of the preferential and unsecured creditors. The statement will give the purchaser a range of likely asset values to be used in subsequent negotiations; it will give an indication as to the likely priorities of the insolvency practitioner; and it will enable the purchaser to gauge the available security value if he requires to borrow money to help fund the purchase.

The statement of affairs is therefore a summary of much of the information that is obtained during the course of a full investigation. This document should be borne in mind throughout the information gathering procedures and these are detailed in the next chapter.

Key point summary

- The purchaser should treat any information obtained from the company's management with caution.
- There will probably be very little time in which to conduct the investigation.
- The purchaser should prepare an estimated statement of affairs for the target company.

7   The detailed investigation

This chapter sets down some guidelines for the potential purchaser of a company as to the questions that should be asked and the information that should be requested about the business, the assets and the liabilities of a company when conducting a full, detailed investigation. If the business and assets only of a company are being acquired, the procedures should be tailored accordingly.

Pointers will also be given on potential pitfalls which may arise during the investigation. The list will not be exhaustive and it must be remembered that individual circumstances may call for additional lines of enquiry. The important thing to remember is that, in undertaking an investigation into the affairs of a company, one should not adhere too strictly to rigid guidelines. Instead, the people undertaking the investigation should be prepared to be flexible and attempt to get a 'feel' for the company and its underlying business.

For convenience, a summary of this chapter is included as an investigation checklist in the appendices.

General review of the business and operations

The purpose of this section of the investigation is to build up a general picture of the company. It will normally be obtained from discussions with the directors and other senior management of the company.

Most of the information will probably be obtained during an initial interview. It is important to keep this information in mind throughout the whole of the investigation process. The investigating team will most likely find that further details will subsequently come to light. These will serve to amplify, modify or even radically change, the first impressions of the company which were obtained during the initial discussions.

The following topics should be discussed and reviewed during the initial interview:

- the general history of the company
- the current structure of the company and, if applicable, the group
- what the company does and in what geographical area
- the industry in which the company operates and the company's principal competitors
- the corporate strategy of the company's management

Although the company is either formally insolvent or close to insolvency, the directors should also be questioned about their long-term plans for the company, what future changes they had contemplated and how such changes were to come about. It is also important to question the directors about the nature of the company's difficulties and to try to find out why they have arisen. The same questions should also be put, tactfully, to other members of the company's management and to any employees whom the purchaser may meet during the course of the investigation. Their differing views can often be quite illuminating.

During the course of the initial interviews, and during the investigation as a whole, the purchaser should be aiming to identify the principal strengths and weaknesses of the company and to assess any potential benefits which may arise out of the proposed acquisition. These important points should be summarised in the final written report.

The previous performance of the company

Assuming that the company has been in existence for a reasonable period of time, the audited accounts are an obvious place to start any review of the previous performance of the company. The accounts can be obtained from the directors of the company or from the insolvency practitioner if one is involved. In such a case, it is likely that some sort of sales document will have been prepared which will usually include a set of the most recent audited accounts and, perhaps, a summary of the accounts or results over the last few years. If copies of the accounts are not readily available, they can be obtained by carrying out a search of the company's file at Companies House. The whole file can be obtained, most easily in microfiche form, either directly from Companies House or from one of the many company search agencies.

The review of the statutory accounts and the rest of the file at Companies House will also identify changes in directors and shareholders and any charges registered against the company and, consequently, any changes in the company's bankers. The directors' information filed at Companies House will also reveal other directorships which they may hold.

The statutory accounts of the company will actually provide little in the way of detailed information but they should indicate general trends in the company's performance. Hence, it should be possible for the purchaser to try to identify some of the likely reasons behind the company's predicament, which can then be confirmed by later discussions with the directors. Of far more use than the statutory accounts will be the detailed accounts prepared for management use or those which have been prepared for tax purposes. These are not usually filed at Companies House and can only be obtained from the company.

The following information should be extracted from the accounts if possible:

- changes in the level of turnover
- changes in gross profit and gross profit percentage
- changes in the level of overheads
- material increases or decreases in fixed assets (by category)
- changes in the levels of current assets and liabilities particularly stock and work in progress, debtors, trade creditors and bank overdraft
- changes in long-term funding
- changes in reserves, particularly revaluation reserves

In virtually all cases, however, the information which can be obtained from the accounts will be limited by the fact that the accounts are, by their nature, out of date, occasionally by several years, and the information is only a summary of the detailed information which is required.

Further information should be requested from the company's management to enable the purchaser to build up a more detailed analysis of the historical results of the company, as shown by the statutory accounts, and in order to cover the period from the date of the last statutory accounts to the date of the investigation. This detailed information should cover a period of at least three years prior to the investigation and should enable the purchaser to schedule monthly sales for the period, broken down between different products or product groups and different customer groups or geographical areas, if possible. From this information, the purchaser should be able to identify any seasonal or other trends in the pattern of sales.

Similar schedules should also be obtained or prepared in respect of cost of sales (broken down between materials, labour and overheads) and gross profit. Ideally, these schedules should be matched with the sales analyses which have been prepared although, in most companies, this will not be easily achieved and the purchaser will have to rely on a general overview. The purpose of this comparison of sales and cost of sales by product line is to try to identify the contribution, or gross profit, which each product or group of products is making for the company, thereby identifying those products which are contributing least to the company's profitability. The purchaser may even find that certain products are being produced at a gross loss with the sales price of the product being insufficient to cover the basic cost of manufacture of the product. Such loss-making products may be concealed if a detailed breakdown of cost of sales is not available.

The investigation should review the company's costing procedures, where applicable, and check their adequacy and accuracy. The investigators should also prepare detailed analyses of the company's overheads, again for a three-year period, and note any trends for subsequent discussion with management.

The conclusion of the detailed review of the accounts should be a calculation of the break-even point for the company. In the case of many troubled companies, this calculation invariably reveals that dramatic increases in sales, or a drastic reduction on overheads, must be achieved for the company to return to profitability.

Accounting systems

Details of the company's basic accounting systems will need to be obtained from the in-house accountant or financial director and an opinion formed of their likely relevance and efficiency. It is a sad fact that many smaller companies in particular are struggling to come to terms with an inappropriate or ineffective computerised accounting system when a manual system would achieve better results and be more easily understood by the company's management. If the company uses computer-based systems, the report should note the software packages in use.

It is important for the purchaser to note whether the information produced by the accounting system is up to date. It is no good reviewing schedules of debtors and creditors which are weeks, or even months, out of date, particularly in the case of a company in trouble.

If the purchaser is intending to bring the company into a group or to absorb it into an existing operation, he needs to start planning how the accounting or reporting functions could be brought into line. It is also relevant to note the stage to which the company's staff prepare accounting records before passing the information to a third party, such as the company's accountants, for final accounts preparation.

Certain accounting functions may be undertaken by third parties and this fact should also be noted. In smaller companies, the auditors may be involved in the preparation of management accounts, VAT returns or payroll or the company may use a payroll bureau.

Accounting information

Many companies produce some form of accounting information on a regular basis although it is surprising how many small and medium sized companies do not. Where such information is prepared, it can vary from pages of very detailed management accounts to a simple statement of sales for the month or the quarter with, perhaps, a list of the company's debtors and creditors. If management accounts are available, they are often produced by external accountants, usually the company's auditors.

It is important to find out precisely what management information is available, how often it is produced, by whom and to whom it is made available. This last point will give some indications as to the decision-making processes existing within the company.

Copies of the management accounting information should be obtained, especially for periods since the last statutory accounts. The information should also be obtained for prior periods where the information is more detailed than that included in the statutory accounts (sales by product line or by branch, for example). The reliability of the management accounting information should also be checked by comparing the information with the previous audited accounts of the company.

Company forecasts

The various forecasts prepared by the company should include sales and trading forecasts, profit projections and cash flow forecasts. In many small and medium sized companies, such forecasts are rarely or never prepared. If a company is in difficulties, the company's bankers will probably have requested at least a cash flow forecast. But such a document is often only prepared annually, as a requirement of the review of the overdraft facility, and is then quickly ignored by the management of the company.

If such documents are in existence, the investigators should obtain copies of the various forecasts, both for future periods and prior periods. The assumptions underlying the forecasts should be noted and their reasonableness should be reviewed. The previous forecasts, when compared with actual results, will demonstrate the reliability of the company's forecasting procedures. It is important to note how the company's forecasts are actually and formally approved by the directors and how the forecasts are monitored against actual performance. If such monitoring is carried out by the company, the investigation should examine the extent to which forecasts are revised.

Where forecasts are not prepared by the company, the investigators will be left with no alternative but to prepare them. Detailed forecasts should be prepared for the first year, with abridged versions for at least the next two or three years. The purchaser should also prepare a set of forecasts which incorporate any changes which he is contemplating after the acquisition.

The company's projected cash flow forecast should be compared with the existing overdraft facility and all the forecasts should be subjected to at least a degree of sensitivity analysis. A simple computer-based model should suffice.

Subsidiaries and other connected companies

The ownership, management, nature and place of business of any subsidiary companies should be identified together with similar information for any companies which may be connected with the target company, for example by virtue of common shareholders or directors. The directors should also be questioned about the reasons behind any acquisition of a subsidiary or association with a connected company. The company search will have revealed other directorships held by the directors of the company and the directors should specifically be questioned about these other companies.

Enquiries should be made about whether any subsidiaries or connected companies operate independently or under the control of the target company. Particular attention should be paid to any intercompany accounts, such as loan accounts, trading accounts and investment accounts, along with any inter-company management charges or dividend payments.

The content and nature of the inter-company accounts should be reviewed and details obtained of the last reconciliation of the accounts. The management of many companies often regard these 'internal' transactions as less important than transactions with third parties. For this reason, problems are often encountered, particularly with inter-company trading accounts, with reconciliations performed perhaps only annually by the company's auditors as part of the audit procedures.

The investigation should obtain copies of the accounts of any subsidiaries or connected companies and compare the level of 'investment' (either by way of trading account or more formal investment) with the present market value of any such companies. When investigating a group of troubled companies, it is surprising how often an inter-company 'asset' balance in one company is shown at full value and is matched by an unsecured creditor balance in the second company, and yet the second company is totally insolvent and there is no possibility whatsoever of the unsecured creditors being paid in full.

The investigation team should also note the existence of any inter-company guarantees at this point and calculate their effect on the individual companies within the group. Again, it is surprising how much the solvency or otherwise of companies within a group can change once the effect of inter-company guarantees has been carefully examined.

Banking arrangements

The bankers to the target company, and other companies connected with it, should be identified and details obtained of all facilities granted by the bank together with details of any security given by the company to the bank, such as debentures, charges, mortgages and guarantees. The guarantees may cover not only guarantees given by the directors of the company or other third parties but also guarantees given to or from connected companies (cross guarantees).

The directors should also be questioned about recent discussions with the company's bankers, especially about any terms for continued support which may have been imposed by the bank. The overdraft facilities which have been granted to the company by the bank should be compared with the future funding requirements taken from the cash flow forecasts.

The team should note any long-term borrowings and prepare schedules detailing such information as:

- the period of the loan
- the interest rate applied
- any security given

It is also important to note the degree to which any loan repayments are in arrears and, at the same time, note any arrears of dividend payments on share capital (such as preference shares).

Management

The purchaser should obtain a copy of the company's formal management organi-sation chart, or prepare one himself if one does not exist. It is important to identify, not only the principal decision maker within the company, but also the other key members of the management or staff. The chart should be accompanied by details of their particular skill or discipline, together with their length of service and, where appropriate, details of their previous experience. Ideally, this information should be built up into a brief, curriculum vitae for each key member of staff.

The purchaser should obtain details of the remuneration packages given to all key employees, including details of any benefits provided by the company and any pension arrangements which may exist. Often directors or other key employ-ees will have service contracts with the company and it is important to obtain copies of these contracts and to schedule any important clauses.

The directors should also be questioned about any key personnel who may have left in the last six months or so and the reasons for their departures. Questions should also be asked about any key personnel who are expected to leave or retire in the foreseeable future.

With this information to hand, the potential purchaser of the business should have a good picture of the company's management, both in terms of style and ability, and he should have identified any possible deficiencies.

Employees and staff

Apart from the key personnel already discussed, details of all other personnel should be obtained in summary form for each of the company's locations, broken down between production staff (both skilled and unskilled), ancillary staff such as transport and stores staff, and administrative staff. The details should include the present staffing levels together with any redundancies which may have been made over the last six months, and any redundancies which may have been planned for the future by the company's management.

Other information which should be obtained is detailed in the investigation checklist included in the appendices but particular attention should be paid to:

- details of any recognised trade unions
- current rates of pay
- recent and imminent pay awards
- terms and conditions of employment

A potential purchaser should be particularly concerned with details of the com-pany's pension scheme. If a pension scheme exists and a substantial number of employees are to be taken over, the purchaser should give serious consideration to obtaining independent, professional advice about the scheme. If the scheme is severely under-funded when it is taken over by a purchaser of the company or business, the sum required to correct any under-funding may, in extreme circum-stances, be out of all proportion to the total purchase consideration paid for the whole company.

It is also important to note all of the relevant details where self-employed personnel are a significant factor in the company's operations. In particular, the purchaser should ascertain that, where arrangements are in force to make gross payments to individuals, correct Inland Revenue procedures are being followed by the company and that the appropriate returns are being made to the Inland Revenue.

Sales and marketing

The purchaser should obtain or prepare appropriate analyses of the company's sales, dependent upon the ability of the company's management systems to provide the information, for a period of at least three years prior to the investigation. Ideally, the sales should be broken down by product or product group and by geographical area. It is also important to note the proportion of turnover which is attributable to the company's major customers. The analyses will provide indications of any expanding or declining markets and will show to what extent the company is reliant on any one customer or a small group of customers.

The marketing strategy should be discussed with the management, including the bases used by the company to determine the sales price of the goods or services which are being sold. Any recent or imminent price increases should be noted and the purchaser should check that these increases have been incorporated into the company's forecasts. The existing discount structure for customers should be noted and whether or not certain customers, or groups of customers, receive preferential discount rates.

If the company uses an invoicing or debt-factoring scheme, the investigators should note the details of the scheme and review any reconciliations of the accounts. It is important for the purchaser to note any significant sales which are being made by the company which are not covered by the scheme and the reasons for this should be established.

The purchaser should review and summarise the company's current order book and comparisons should be made with prior periods, if this is possible, in order to establish the extent to which the company's market is expanding or contracting. For similar reasons, the purchaser should discuss with management the likely impact that any changes in technology, increased competition and so on, could have on the company's turnover.

The purchaser should also review any deposits received from customers and discuss the rationale behind them. The purchaser should enquire whether the company has obtained any insurance cover in respect of these deposits or whether the deposits are placed in a trust account until they can legitimately be used by the company. If the business and assets of a company are being acquired from an insolvency practitioner, the purchaser should consider the likely impact of honouring any pre-insolvency orders where deposits have been taken by the company and where the purchaser will be unable to get credit for such deposits.

Purchasing

The purchaser should obtain details of the principal suppliers to the company, together with details of any recent, or imminent price rises. If any forward purchasing contacts exist, details should be obtained and summarised.

In the case of a company in trouble, the company will probably have changed its suppliers because of a lack of available credit. Similarly, delayed payments to creditors may have resulted in purchase discounts not being obtained or even penalty interest rates being applied by creditors. All these factors should be noted by the purchaser as they could have an impact on the valuation of stock, where the company's stock is effectively being overvalued because of the unnecessarily higher prices which the company has been forced into paying.

The purchaser should find out whether the company has experienced difficulties in obtaining supplies in the past, especially where such delays have resulted in reduced or delayed production or sales. The reasons for such difficulties should be established, particularly as to whether the difficulties were caused by the company (such as a lack of available credit) or by the supplier (the supplier simply could not supply).

Production/work in progress

This part of the investigation will be highly specific to the particular company concerned. However, certain general guidelines can be laid down which will be applicable to most manufacturing concerns. In the first place, the purchaser should prepare a general description of the manufacturing process.

The purchaser should interview the appropriate personnel to find out whether goods are produced to order or, if not, whether the current production work is identifiable to known and current customers of the company. The interview should establish the method of determining the company's production programme and the personnel involved in this procedure.

The interview should also determine if significant amounts of work are placed with outside subcontractors and the ownership of any dies and tools involved in such work should be checked. In certain circumstances, it will also be relevant to ascertain the amounts outstanding to such subcontractors to see whether they could effectively hold the company to ransom.

Supplementary questions applicable in certain cases will include:

- the average production timescale
- the changeover time where short production runs are involved
- procedures for measuring costs to date against estimates

It will be important to note whether there is any spare production capacity and whether or not such spare capacity is a result of production constraints such as:

- seasonality of customer orders
- shortage of raw materials
- ability or shortage of personnel
- suitability or reliability of production machinery

If the company is involved in long-term contracts, the purchaser should establish the policies used by the company in taking profits on the contracts. If the purchaser is considering taking over the contracts or having them novated, he should review any further monies receivable under the contracts and compare such monies with the likely costs of completing the contracts.

Land and buildings

The report should list details of the company's freehold, leasehold and rented property. These details will include, for each property:

- general description of the property
- original cost plus the costs of any additions to the property
- copies of any valuations obtained by the company, including valuations for insurance purposes
- details of the company's tenure of the property including copies of leases or rental agreements if appropriate
- details of any tenants together with copies of the relevant leases

All properties should be visually inspected wherever possible so that the present condition of the properties can be ascertained and whether or not there is any surplus space available which could be better utilised or sold off. Such visits will also enable the potential purchaser to record whether or not any of the properties are shared with other companies and, if so, whether any segregation is possible. This segregation may also apply to separate divisions of the target company, where the purchaser is contemplating either the purchase of only part of the company, or to the resale of part of the company after the purchase of the whole.

Discussions should also be held concerning possible alternative uses of the company's properties, or future improvements which may have been planned, together with the current planning status of all of the properties. Enquiries should also be made about any transfer or conveyance of property either to or from the company which is in progress.

In due course, the company's legal title to any properties will need to be checked to ensure that title is not held by connected companies or persons (such as directors or shareholders) or other third parties.

Although copies of any property valuations will have been obtained, serious consideration should be given to obtaining new valuations on all significant properties. Even if valuations have been obtained recently by the company, property valuations can vary considerably within a relatively short period of time, depending upon the current economic climate. Moreover, it is only when instructions are given to a professional valuer that the precise basis of the valuation can be determined. The purchaser should be looking for two bases of valuation for each property; a valuation based upon the open market value in its present use and condition and a forced sale, 'bricks and mortar' valuation. The latter valuation is the one relevant to anyone who is to provide funds to the purchaser for the acquisition. It would be prudent to ensure that any valuer employed by the purchaser is acceptable to such a lender.

Plant, machinery, vehicles, office furniture and equipment

Enquiries should first of all be made about any existing inventory or register of such fixed assets. If the purchaser is buying from an insolvency practitioner, he will probably have had prepared a list of at least the principal fixed assets of the company. A schedule of the cost and associated depreciation of relevant assets should be prepared, if necessary in summary form by category of asset, and the schedule should be cross-referenced to a schedule of finance agreements where appropriate.

The visit to the company's premises will enable the purchaser to determine the age and condition of, at least, the principal assets. Very specialised assets should also be noted. Such assets may not be particularly attractive to third parties and will attract a comparatively low valuation. Any significant items on loan either to or from the company should also be noted.

The investigators should interview the directors about significant recent capital expenditure together with details of future, planned expenditure including those items which may already have been contracted for.

It is possible that the directors have obtained a valuation of the company's fixed assets, in which case the purchaser should obtain a copy, together with details of the basis and purpose of the valuation. It is more than likely that a valuation will not have been obtained and the purchaser will have to rely as a starting point on the estimates of book value collected during the investigation.

It is rare for a purchaser to contemplate a professional valuation of the company's fixed assets, although circumstances will exist where this should be considered, for example, where such assets are both significant and highly specialised. Provided the current depreciation policies of the company are seen to be reasonable, the book values of the fixed assets will give a good indication as to the likely going concern values of such assets, particularly after making due allowance for the other information which will have been established during the course of the investigation and the purchaser's likely knowledge and experience of the business. Advice should also be taken from any advisors who may be assisting the purchaser.

After taking appropriate advice, the forced sale value of the fixed assets will represent the likely value attributable to such assets in a forced sale or auction. In general terms, in order to arrive at such forced sale values, the write down of fixed assets will need to be significant, often by as much as 50 per cent or even 75 per cent, and particularly in the case of computers and specialised items of plant and machinery.

Assets under finance or rental agreements

All assets which are under any hire purchase, leasing or other finance agreement should be identified and copies of the relevant agreements obtained. Similarly, with any assets which are being rented by the company.

A schedule should be obtained or prepared, grouped by finance or rental company, to show:

- a description of the asset
- the date of purchase and the length of the agreement
- the original purchase price and the 'financed' amount
- any arrears outstanding under the agreements
- future amounts payable under the agreement

The schedule should be cross-referenced to the fixed assets schedules and estimates of current realisable value thus obtained. A simple extension will then allow the purchaser to calculate the potential equity, or otherwise, available to the company in such assets. In due course, the calculation should be refined by obtaining actual settlement figures from the finance companies concerned. Unfortunately, there is a current trend for many fixed assets, especially motor vehicles, to be obtained quite easily on leasing agreements, with little or no initial deposit being paid, with the result that there is little or no equity available for the company or a subsequent purchaser.

Wherever possible, the assets covered by the schedule of finance agreements should be physically inspected and the schedule should also be cross-referenced to a schedule of direct debits, or similar, showing payments being made by the company. Although illegal, it is not by any means unknown for a company in trouble to dispose of assets under finance agreements in order to raise much needed working capital, then not to inform the finance company concerned, for obvious reasons, and simply to continue paying the monthly or quarterly instalments.

Intangible assets

Enquiries should be made about any intangible assets or intellectual property rights which may be available to a prospective purchaser. These may include such items as licence agreements, patents and trade-marks.

Particular attention should be paid to the precise ownership of intellectual property. There are occasions when disputes do arise with regard to ownership and a purchaser would do well to clarify any problem areas prior to acquisition rather than become involved in expensive litigation afterwards.

The valuation of intangible assets or intellectual property may well present the purchaser with a problem and third-party assistance may be required, particularly in respect of assets that have not previously been included in the company's balance sheet.

Any goodwill existing in the books of the company will have arisen on the previous acquisition of another business or company or upon the incorporation of a pre-existing business. It will refer to the extent to which the price paid for the assets of the business or company exceeded the book value of those assets.

The investigators should discuss the reasons for the existence of any goodwill with the management of the company together with the company's policy for writing it off over a period of time. In all but the most exceptional cases, any goodwill existing in the books of the troubled company will have no value for a purchaser of the company.

Stock

The investigators should prepare a summary of the stock held at each business location, broken down, for example between raw materials, component or stores stock and finished goods. The schedule may also be analysed between different product groups or categories and should also attempt to allocate, for each stock category, any slow-moving, redundant or obsolete stock.

In certain types of business, the company may work on certain materials which are issued by the customer at no charge. It is important to obtain full details of such free issue stock and, similarly, any stock held on a 'sale or return' basis.

The investigation should establish the method of valuing the company's stock and, as policies change from time to time, the timing and details of any change in valuation method. The purchaser should also calculate the rate of the company's stock turnover, analysed again if possible between different products or product groups.

The way that stock is counted can vary from company to company, usually dependent upon the size and nature of the stock holding and whether or not a stock control system is being operated by the company. Such a system could be either a manual, usually card-based, system or, more likely in the present age, a computer-based system. Where a stock control system is in operation, the entire stock holding may never be counted at the same time. Instead, checks are usually made against the stock system, perhaps on a department by department basis. In smaller companies, the entire stock holding may be counted only once a year as part of the annual audit procedures. Alternatively, there are still instances of physical stock counts never being performed, with the annual valuation of stock for accounts purposes being based entirely upon directors' valuations.

The particular circumstances of the target company will dictate whether or not a detailed stock count will be required by a prospective purchaser. In the case of a purchase of a troubled company where stock is a significant item, a physical stock count is imperative. When a company is in difficulties, the usually balanced stock holding is often the first to suffer; supplies become more difficult to obtain, stock holdings are depleted and the residual stock may consist almost entirely of slow-moving or obsolete stock. Notwithstanding this fact, it would be usual for a potential purchaser to rely upon the company's stock records or other broad assumptions for the valuation of stock during the investigation procedures and for the detailed physical counting and subsequent valuation of the whole stock holding to be part of the procedures involved in the completion of a subsequent sale contract.

During the initial investigation, enquiries should be made about how often physical stock counts are performed and, if a stock control system is being used, the recent results of comparing any physical counts with the stock records. Similar enquiries should also be made about the company's policy with regard to slow-moving or obsolete stock and the provisions associated with such stock.

Occasionally, instances may be found where the company has entered into some form of stock financing agreement. Such details should be noted and a copy of the relevant agreements obtained.

If the purchaser is planning to buy from an insolvency practitioner, in particular, he should have regard to possible claims for reservation, or retention, of title against the company's stock by unsecured creditors of the company. Any major groups or types of stock should be identified where this could be a potential problem. This subject is discussed more fully in the next chapter.

For the purpose of the investigation, the going concern valuation of the stock should have regard to the level of slow-moving or obsolete stock and the degree to which a purchaser could perhaps have purchased the stock on more favourable terms. In order to arrive at a forced sale valuation, due consideration will have to be paid to such factors as the degree of specialisation of the stock and the fact that, for most purposes, it is now classed as 'used' or second-hand stock. The general state of the market place for such stock may also be a relevant factor.

Debtors

The investigation team should first obtain a current aged list of debtors and should prepare a summary.

If the company uses a computerised sales ledger, the resultant aged list of debtors should be scrutinised most carefully. Particular attention should be paid to such items as unallocated cash and credit balances, together with any 'control' accounts which may be included in the ledger, such as cash sales, staff sales and sundry sales. After making adjustments for such items, the actual ageing of the debtors can alter substantially. Allowances should also be made for any subsidiary or connected company balances which should be excluded from the aged analysis and scheduled separately.

The investigators should identify major customers, detailing year-to-date turnover if such is possible, together with an analysis of the numbers of remaining debtors, prepared in selected ranges of debt. A further analysis should identify any debtors who are also creditors of the company and the 'net' position should be established in respect of these accounts.

The team should examine the company's record of bad debts and prepare an analysis of the existing reserves or provisions for bad and doubtful debts. In particular, the analysis should be compared with the older debts in the aged listing of debtors and details and explanations obtained for any debts which have not been provided for.

Details and explanations should also be obtained for any major debts where the history of the debt appears to be unusual, such as where isolated monthly balances appear or where round sum payments on account are being made. Such accounts could again indicate areas where further provisions are required.

The investigators should review the company's files of correspondence with credit agencies or solicitors involved in debt collection work and note details of the general debt collection history and any major specific disputes with debtors.

Although it is not allowable under the VAT legislation, instances are occasionally found where bad debts are written off the sales ledger by the use of credit notes and credit notes over a suitable period should be reviewed. Such a review may also provide an indication of such matters as the quality of the company's accounting or invoicing procedures (by reference to credit notes being issued for short deliveries or invoicing errors) and the quality of the manufacturing process (where credit notes are being issued for returns or faulty workmanship). The company's credit terms should be established both for major customers and for all other customers. Any exceptions to the normal credit terms should also be noted.

The purchaser should obtain details of any product warranties or other guarantees which may be provided to customers by the company and establish the details of the history of any claims under such warranties or guarantees. Similar details should be obtained if the company provides any after-sales service for any products.

The company's credit control procedures should answer the following queries:

- what status checks are made on new customers?
- who authorises the setting up of new accounts?
- is a 'stop' list used and, if so, how often is it updated?
- what internal, chasing procedures are used?
- when are outstanding debtors referred to outside agencies such as solicitors or debt collection agencies?

Where the company pays commission to salesmen or representatives, it is useful at this stage to establish the details and method of calculation of such commission, such as whether it is based upon sales to customers or cash received from customers.

The purchaser should review any sundry debtors and prepayments and pay particular attention to any significant items, especially 'one-off' items such as insurance claims and the like.

Any amounts due to the company from the directors should be carefully reviewed. The purchaser should enquire about the reasons behind such debts and should note any recent, significant changes. He should also take advice about the legality of, and potential tax liability arising on, these debts.

The review of the company's debtors should enable the purchaser to take the gross value of the debtors and to make suitable adjustments in order to arrive at the likely going concern value. These adjustments will include, not only specific provisions for known or likely bad or disputed debtors, but also general provisions relating to the age of the older debtors and costs such as warranty or guarantee claims associated with the general collection of debtors. The cost of collection of debtors will also have particular relevance to certain classifications of debtors, such as retentions, where the anticipated costs associated with the collection of outstanding debts may well be significant.

In trying to establish a suitable forced sale value for the company's debtors, the purchaser is trying to establish the value which such debtors may realise in a 'close-down' situation. Thus significant provisions will need to be made for such items as contract debtors, where the completion of the contract will not be possible and counterclaims may well arise, or other debtors where there is a likelihood that counterclaims may arise for bad or faulty workmanship and the like. In other words, it is highly probable that a better realisation will be achieved from debtors arising from the sale of wholesale confectionery products, where it would be difficult for the customer to dispute the debt, than would be the case from a sales ledger consisting of debts due in respect of general building works, where it can be almost guaranteed that every debt will be disputed.

Cash and investments

In many companies, the amount of cash on hand will not be significant. Where this is not the case, however, due attention should be paid to the cut-off with regard to the bank account, stock or debtors.

In the case of investments, a schedule should be prepared detailing the general description of the holding, the cost and current market value and, where appropriate, any terms of repayment.

If any insurance policies exist where the company is a beneficiary, appropriate details and surrender values should be obtained.

Preferential creditors

In general terms, the principal preferential creditors arising on the formal insolvency of a company are as follows:

- Inland Revenue in respect of PAYE income tax (and subcontractor deductions in the building or construction industry) arising in the 12 months prior to the insolvency
- Department of Social Security in respect of National Insurance contributions for a similar period of 12 months
- Customs and Excise in respect of value added tax arising in the six months prior to the insolvency
- employees' arrears of pay and holiday pay claims, subject to certain limits

If amounts due to preferential creditors exceed the time or other limits noted above, the balance of the individual creditors' claim is unsecured.

Preferential creditor claims should be calculated together with the periods to which they relate. Copies of the relevant statutory returns for previous periods should also be obtained. In particular, details should be obtained where the company forms part of a group registration for VAT purposes. If the company is the representative member for the purpose of such a group registration, the purchaser will need to obtain details of the liability in respect of other group members.

The directors should be questioned about the last visit to the company's premises by both the Inland Revenue and Customs and Excise. If arrangements have been made for the payment of any arrears to any government department, details should be noted together with comments as to whether or not the arrangement has been adhered to.

The purchaser should prepare a summary schedule of amounts due to employees in respect of arrears of pay and holiday pay.

Unsecured creditors

An aged analysis of trade and expense creditors should be obtained and a summary prepared. Particular attention should be paid to the principal suppliers to the company.

The investigators should note the internal systems for the recording and authorization of purchases, particularly the systems relating to accounting provisions for goods received by the company, but not yet invoiced, and accrued expenses. They should also note any payments to creditors which have not yet passed through the company's bank account. Occasionally, situations can be found where a company adopts a policy of writing out a large number of cheques for suppliers, perhaps once a month, and then sending out the cheques as and when funds are available. The writing back of such cheques will usually have a significant effect on the extent of the company's creditors.

If loan creditors are involved, details of the conditions and terms of the loans should be noted and copies of the loan agreements obtained if significant. If loans have been made to the company by the directors, details should be obtained of any movements on such accounts over the last 12 months.

Creditors arising from the company's sales ledger should not be overlooked. These may include routine credit balances arising from overpayments from customers or payments in advance from customers.

The purchaser should prepare a summary schedule of the likely amounts due to the company's employees in respect of payments in lieu of notice and redundancy payments.

Since it is a troubled company under investigation, the directors or other officials should be carefully questioned about any of the following:

- any statutory demands received by the company from creditors
- any writs which have been received by the company and, in particular, those which are still unsatisfied
- any actual or potential distraints on any of the company's assets
- any walking possession orders
- any winding-up petitions which may have been received (it is not unusual for such to be hidden in a drawer and forgotten!)

The purchaser should also question the directors about any meetings or discussions which may have been held with any of the company's major creditors concerning the payment of outstanding debts. He should obtain details of any arrangements which may have been agreed and whether such arrangements have been adhered to.

Taxation

Apart from the preferential creditors which have already been mentioned, details should be obtained of any corporation tax which may be payable, including any capital gains tax. The directors or, where possible, the company's accountants should be questioned about the taxation affairs of the company in general, with particular regard to any capital or trading losses which could be available to a purchaser of the company or business.

Conclusion of the investigation

The investigation process will produce a wealth of information about the company and this should be consolidated into a formal written report. Even if the investigation has been minimal and undertaken personally by the potential purchaser, the preparation of a written report will help both to isolate the important factors which are involved in the purchase and to highlight the strengths and weaknesses of the proposed acquisition.

Key point summary

- The detailed investigation procedures should be tailored to fit the particular circumstances.
- The investigation should conclude with the preparation of a written report. The principal headings of a full investigation report should be as follows:
  - objectives of report
  - brief history of the company
  - accounting history for, say, the previous five years
  - current trading position
  - future trading prospects
  - current financial position
  - principal strengths and weaknesses of the company
  - likely tangible and intangible benefits arising from the proposed acquisition
  - conclusions and recommendations

  Appendices will then deal with:
  - the statement of estimated financial position
  - brief curriculum vitae for key employees
  - summaries of detailed information
  - copies of accounts
  - copies of important documents

8   What about assets that do not belong to the company?

Assets under finance

The investigation process should have identified assets under hire purchase, leasing and other finance contracts. Such assets do not belong to the target company but to the company that supplied the finance for their purchase.

If a company is being purchased from the shareholders, the situation is relatively straightforward; the new owner of the business will simply inherit the existing obligations of the acquired company to the finance companies concerned. Furthermore, the previous owners will probably want the purchaser of the company to take over any personal obligations to finance companies, such as guarantees.

There may well be cases, of course, where excessive finance obligations will preclude the purchase of the shares of a company, either because the assets concerned are no longer required by the company, or because the type and, particularly, the cost of the specific forms of finance agreements are out of all proportion to their benefit. Once a finance contract is signed, the company has to pay for the asset until the end of the contractual period. Alternatively where a sale is possible under the terms of the agreement, the asset could be sold and the finance company repaid out of the sale proceeds, sometimes with a penalty payment for early termination of the contract.

If financed assets are no longer required or are not being used effectively by a company, their sale may result in a contractual liability to the finance companies concerned far in excess of their realisable value. Alternatively, the company may have no right to sell the assets concerned and will therefore have no alternative but to continue the payments until the contract is completed.

If the business and assets are being purchased from an insolvency practitioner, the sale agreement will probably exclude any assets which are not owned by the company. Occasionally, hire purchase or leased assets may be included in a sale, with the insolvency practitioner subsequently paying off any outstanding liability to the finance company concerned. The purchaser should be wary in such cases; under most finance contracts, the title to the asset in question will not pass to the company until some future point in time or not at all. If the company has not got adequate title to the asset, the insolvency practitioner cannot give good title to a purchaser. Thus, the purchaser may be paying for something he cannot own!

In certain cases, assets under finance contracts may be dealt with by separate negotiations between the insolvency practitioner and the purchaser. The insolvency practitioner will have undertaken an exercise in relation to all financed assets where the estimated realisable values of the assets will have been obtained, usually from professional advisors, together with details of the amounts required by the finance companies concerned in order to settle the outstanding obligations under the agreements. The insolvency practitioner will therefore have calculated any equity which may be available in the financed assets and which could be realised for the benefit of the company's creditors. Even where, under the original finance agreement, the company could never acquire any right to dispose of the particular asset, such a right may usually be granted in an insolvency.

If a purchaser wishes to take over or acquire any of the company's financed assets, he will first need to reach agreement with the insolvency practitioner for the payment of any equity in the assets. Usually, this will simply be a matter of negotiation between the two parties. However, situations may arise where a finance company has a number of finance agreements with the insolvent company, perhaps several different types of agreement, and will only agree to deal with any relevant assets on the basis that all the agreements are transferred to, or all the relevant assets are sold to, a new party. If this is not acceptable, the finance company will repossess the assets in question.

The reason for this attitude is obvious; the finance company does not want to be left only with assets on which significant losses will be incurred in subsequent realisations. This consolidation of finance agreements is common practice in dealings between finance companies and insolvency practitioners during the course of administrative receiverships. However it may be possible for a subsequent purchaser of the business and assets of an insolvent company to reach a reasonable settlement, and on individual assets if necessary, by negotiating with both the insolvency practitioner and the finance company concerned.

Thus, the purchaser of the business and assets of a company will have several available options available in respect of any financed assets; if the asset in question is not required in the new company, the purchaser need take no further action and the finance company will remove and dispose of the asset in due course. Alternatively after negotiating payment of any equity to the insolvency practitioner, the purchaser can either take over the existing contract between the old company and the finance company or purchase the asset in question from the finance company.

If the purchaser wishes to take over the existing finance contract, the finance company will expect to get the agreement of the original company, acting through the insolvency practitioner, to the transfer. Although, it is difficult to see any circumstances where such agreement would not be given, provided any equity has been paid to the insolvency practitioner, it is as well to obtain the specific agreement of the insolvency practitioner, in the contract for the sale of the business and assets for example, that full cooperation will be given in the transfer of any finance agreements to the purchaser.

As an alternative to taking over the finance contract for the old company, the purchaser has the option of purchasing the asset directly from the finance company. If a finance company repossesses an asset, it will want to dispose of it as soon as possible for the best possible price, in order to mitigate its loss. In cases where little deposit was paid by the old company at the start of the contract, or where the asset in question is very specialised, or in a period of recession, the realisable value of the asset is likely to be very much less than the outstanding liability to the finance company and a purchaser could acquire a very reasonably priced asset, especially when compared with the alternative of taking over the existing contract. This course of action should most definitely be considered, if the purchaser has surplus funds available.

The purchaser should, of course, take account of the cost of acquiring a similar asset elsewhere, and the cost of delivery and installation, before making an offer to a finance company.

Assets subject to reservation of title

The question of reservation, or retention, of title is considered here to ensure that the purchaser can obtain good title for assets which are sold to him. A reservation of title clause in a sales contract is also known as a *Romalpa* clause, after the case which first highlighted the subject.

Under the Sale of Goods Act 1979, the title or ownership in any goods which are being sold usually passes from the seller to the buyer when the goods are delivered to the buyer. A reservation of title clause in a sales contract is an attempt by the seller to retain title in the goods after they have been delivered, until the goods have been paid for.

The question of reservation of title usually applies to goods bought for resale (such as stock, for example) but it can also apply to capital equipment. If many suppliers of goods or other assets to a company do have valid reservation of title claims, the insolvency practitioner may be trying to sell the business and assets of the company which has no assets to dispose of!

If suppliers to the company have already proved that they have valid reservation of title claims to stock or other assets of the company, the insolvency practitioner will not be able to give good title in these goods to a purchaser in a subsequent sale of the business. Such goods should be specifically excluded from the sale agreement. The insolvency practitioner should be asked to confirm, in the contract or other binding document, that the sale does not include any assets which are subject to valid reservation of title claims.

From the purchaser's point of view, the situation is then similar to that discussed above in relation to assets under finance agreements; assuming the goods over which reservation of title has been successfully claimed are still physically available to the purchaser, he can negotiate directly with the supplier for the repurchase of the goods. As many suppliers would obviously prefer cash to the return of the goods in question, the purchaser may be able to obtain the goods at a favourable discount. This would be particularly relevant if the goods were specifically made for the original company or otherwise of little use to the supplier.

A problem arises if the insolvency practitioner has been notified of potential reservation of title claims but such claims have not yet been resolved. The tight deadline usually imposed by an insolvency means that the practitioner often faces a potential purchaser with claims unresolved. The problem does not usually occur where assets are being sold to a purchaser of the business at their full cost price; if notified reservation of title claims subsequently prove to be valid, the insolvency practitioner can hand over the cost price of those goods to the supplier. In virtually all cases, however, the goods are being sold to the purchaser at a discount and the insolvency practitioner may find that he has to hand over an amount in excess of the selling price of the goods to any creditor who has a successful reservation of title claim.

The dilemma is that the purchaser wishes to obtain good title to everything which he is buying from the insolvency practitioner. But the insolvency practitioner will not be able to give good title to goods if a claim has been made for potential reservation of title. In practice, commerciality usually prevails and there are several ways out of the predicament. In all cases, the goods in dispute should be identified and a summary appended to the sale contract. The insolvency practitioner should be asked to confirm that, as at the date of the contract, the appended claims are the only claims which have been notified to him and then either:

(a) The goods in question can be excluded from the contract. This will leave the insolvency practitioner to deal with the claims and, if the claims do not prove to be valid, the goods can be disposed of either to the purchaser of the business or to another third party.

(b) The potential claims over the goods can be quantified and sold to the purchaser with the proceeds of sale of the goods in question being placed into a separate fund. The insolvency practitioner can then deal with the reservation of title claims and the balance of the fund will revert to the practitioner in due course. This may well be the cleanest option for the purchaser especially if the goods in question are required for the trade of the company to continue smoothly.

(c) The potential claims over the goods in question can be quantified and an appropriate reduction made in the sale price but, in this case, the purchaser is given possession of the goods and is left to deal with the suppliers concerned. The purchaser will have to indemnify the insolvency practitioner in respect of any claims arising because the purchaser has acquired possession of the goods. This option could be attractive to a purchaser because he will have obtained a discount on the sale price and he can perhaps subsequently negotiate even more favourable terms with the suppliers concerned. Negotiations may well favour the purchaser for:

- the goods may be too specialised to be of use to the supplier
- the supplier will want to settle quickly rather than become involved in possibly protracted legal proceedings
- the supplier may want to maintain the business relationship

The risk for the purchaser is that if he cannot come to a satisfactory deal with the supplier he will have either to pay for the goods in full or return them to the supplier.

There may be alternative methods of dealing with goods potentially subject to reservation of title claims, depending upon the particular circumstances. Such claims invariably arise in every insolvency nowadays and the purchaser, or his solicitor, must ensure that the subject is satisfactorily resolved in the contract.

Although this book is not intended to provide a detailed explanation of reservation of title, it may be useful to summarise the various points on which a creditor must satisfy an insolvency practitioner in order to prove a valid reservation of title claim.

- The reservation of title clause must be included in the contract between the parties to the contract. It is often not enough to have the condition on the bottom, or on the back, of a sales invoice as the invoice usually follows delivery of the goods and the title will already have passed on delivery. However such a condition can be incorporated into a contract if there has been a course of trading over a period of time between the two parties.
- The reservation of title clause must be valid. This will depend upon the precise wording of the clause and is usually a matter for solicitors.
- There must be goods over which the supplier can claim title under the clause. If goods have been purchased from several suppliers, for example, it may be difficult for one creditor to prove that the goods have been supplied by him rather than another supplier.
- Unless the supplier has a valid clause which entitles him to lay claim to any goods which he has supplied, he must be able to prove that the goods in question have not been paid for. If one box of goods which has not been paid for, is placed with other boxes of goods which have been paid for, it may be impossible for the supplier to prove which box is which. On the other hand, if goods are supplied with serial numbers or other markings which are specifically identified on unpaid invoices, identification will be relatively straightforward.
- In general, the goods in dispute must be in their original state and must not have been worked upon by the company or incorporated into something else.

Although the above is intended to be a summary of the various problems relating to reservation of title, it is important to note that the matter is based, to a large extent, upon case law and is therefore subject to change as new cases are decided by the courts. The purchaser must therefore take adequate legal advice on the matter at the time of the proposed acquisition.

Other third-party assets

Apart from assets under finance contracts and assets subject to reservation of title claims, there are potentially other assets which may belong to third parties and which cannot therefore be sold as part of the business and assets of a company. Although usually not of the same significance as assets which are subject to reservation of title claims or assets under finance agreements, the purchaser should pay particular attention to any potential third-party assets during the course of the investigation and he should ensure that such assets are specifically excluded from the contract. Such assets may include:

- assets under rental agreements
- assets being loaned to the company
- assets covered by a 'sale or return' agreement
- customer's own goods

Key point summary

- The purchaser should investigate the possibility of making cash offers to finance companies in respect of assets under hire purchase or leasing agreements.
- The purchaser must ensure that goods subject to potential reservation of title claims are satisfactorily dealt with in the contract.
- The purchaser must ensure that he is fully aware of any other third-party assets on the company's premises, particularly where such assets are vital to the running of the business.

9   What about the employees?

Potential purchasers of insolvent businesses should pay particular attention to the subject of employees. A failure to do so could result in significant and unforeseen liabilities.

Liabilities to employees

In general terms the liabilities of an employer to an employee fall into four categories of which two represent actual liabilities and two are contingent liabilities which arise only when the employee is dismissed. These liabilities are:

- arrears of pay
- accrued holiday pay
- payments in lieu of notice
- redundancy pay

Arrears of pay and holiday pay are normal liabilities of an employer at any point in time and represent time or work done which has not been paid for and accrued holiday pay which has not been taken. A payment in lieu of notice will only become a liability when an employee is dismissed. The employee will be entitled to a period of notice, either written into his contract of employment or implied by statute. In simple terms, the statutory notice period is one week per year of service with a minimum period of two weeks and a maximum period of twelve weeks. Any notice period which is written into an individual contract of employment may well exceed these statutory limits. An employee can either continue to work for the employer during the period of notice or, if he is dismissed without notice, he is entitled to a payment equivalent to what he would have earned during the notice period.

When an employee who has been continuously employed for more than two years is made redundant, he is entitled to statutory redundancy pay. The amount to which he is entitled is calculated by reference to his age and length of service and can be up to a maximum of 30 weeks pay.

All employees have contracts of employment either in writing or implied under the relevant employment legislation. Many employers will have standard contracts of employment for most employees with, perhaps, separate, individual contracts for senior management and directors. A prospective purchaser of a company should be fully aware of all the terms in these contracts of employment.

Employees in a pre-insolvency situation

Where a company is acquired from existing shareholders, the purchaser can do little about the employees. Essentially, the employer (the company) will not have changed and the purchaser will automatically become responsible for all those employees who are in the company's employment at the time of the acquisition. Moreover, the purchaser could find that additional liabilities come to light following the acquisition, for example if the company was being prosecuted for unfair dismissal by an employee who had been dismissed prior to the acquisition.

If, after the acquisition, the purchaser decides not to retain certain employees, the company, and therefore the purchaser, will become liable for any employee claims arising from such redundancies. If employees belong to a recognised trade union, the employer also has a duty to consult with the unions concerned about the proposed redundancies as early as possible.

In the case of the purchase of only the business and assets of a company, prior to a formal insolvency, the purchaser's liabilities to the employees of the old company will be very much as described below in relation to the purchase of the business and assets of a company from an insolvency practitioner. The principal difference is that the insolvency practitioner will probably have made certain redundancies from the workforce during the course of the receivership or administration. Prior to an insolvency, it is quite probable that such redundancies will not have been made. The potential liability of the purchaser will thereby be increased and, in cases where the company is overstaffed, could be significant.

Employees in an insolvency

Where a company is formally insolvent and the business and assets are being purchased as a going concern, the purchaser will most likely find that he is dealing with an insolvency practitioner acting as either an administrative receiver or an administrator. Upon his appointment, the insolvency practitioner will have assessed the ability of the company to continue trading and he will probably have dismissed a number of employees in order to ensure that the continued trading is viable, at least for a short period of time. Indeed, the number of these initial redundancies may well have been significant as a high degree of overstaffing can often be a major contribution to a company's downfall. In such cases, the company's management often wants to make more cutbacks but feels that it cannot afford to do so because of the high costs associated with such redundancies. The company is then in a vicious, and often terminal, circle.

Following the initial dismissals, the liabilities of the insolvent company to the dismissed employees will be paid, up to certain limits, by the Department of Employment out of the National Insurance Fund. The insolvency practitioner will make the appropriate claims to the Department of Employment on behalf of the employees and, after making the payments, the Department will 'stand in the shoes' of the employees with claims against the insolvent company.

If employees are retained during the insolvency, the insolvency practitioner will continue to make company funds available to pay wages and salaries. As the insolvency proceeds, he will probably make further redundancies. However, a point will hopefully be reached where the insolvency practitioner will wish to dispose of the business and assets of the company to a prospective purchaser, as a going concern.

Prior to 1982, when a purchaser acquired the business of an insolvent company, the various liabilities of the company to the employees could not be transferred to a purchaser of the business, as contracts of employment could not be transferred by an employer without the consent of the employees concerned. Thus, all the employees would eventually be dismissed by the insolvency practitioner and all employee claims for arrears of pay, holiday pay, lieu of notice payments and redundancy pay would be paid to the employees by the Department of Employment, even if the employees were all subsequently re-employed by the purchaser of the business.

In 1982, the provisions of the Transfer of Undertakings (Protection of Employment) Regulations 1981 came into force. These regulations broadly state that, where a business is transferred from one person to another, anyone employed by the business immediately prior to the transfer automatically has their contract of employment transferred with the business. Therefore, as the contracts of employment are not terminated, the employees cannot make claims for redundancy pay and other entitlements, and these liabilities, both actual and contingent, fall upon the purchaser of the business. In practice, of course, the principal part of such liabilities, lieu of notice and redundancy payments, would not become payable until the new purchaser of the business made the transferred employees redundant.

In the period since 1982, much of the case law has focused on the point that it is only employees employed by the company *immediately prior to* the transfer of the business who had their contracts transferred. Employees who were dismissed prior to that time would receive their full entitlement to redundancy pay and other entitlements, even if they were subsequently re-employed by the purchaser. This led to a situation where employees would be dismissed only hours before a sale of the business. They would be entitled to receive their redundancy pay and other entitlements, and then would be re-employed by the purchaser immediately after the sale was completed, with no liability whatsoever falling on the new employer.

The effect of the Litster case

Recently the invariable dismissal of all employees just prior to a sale of the business has changed, following an appeal in the House of Lords in March 1989. In the case of Litster and others v. Forth Dry Dock & Engineering Company Limited and another, the House ruled that the various employees' contracts had been transferred to the purchaser of the business.

Thus, when a purchaser is considering acquiring the business of an insolvent company, the insolvency practitioner involved will be unable to give any assurances to the purchaser that the employees' contracts of employment will not be transferred to the purchaser when the sale is completed. In cases where employees' contracts of employment are held to be transferred to a purchaser of the business, any liabilities, both existing and contingent, of the previous company to those employees will be transferred also.

In practice, it is likely that any employees dismissed by the insolvency practitioner immediately after his appointment will not have their contracts of employment transferred to the purchaser, assuming that a reasonable period of time has elapsed before a subsequent sale of the business. Conversely, it is likely that those employees who are still employed at some point between the time when negotiations with a purchaser begin and the time when the sale is concluded, will have their contracts transferred. The Department of Employment will review each case as it arises and the potential purchaser of any business as a going concern should take appropriate legal advice on the matter.

In practical terms, the whole question may not be significant to the purchaser. The workforce may have been trimmed down to an acceptable level at an early stage of the insolvency and the remaining workforce may only have been employed by the original company for a comparatively short period of time. Even if redundancies are made by the purchaser following the acquisition, the financial effect may be minimal.

However, the purchaser may find a situation where the business has not been trimmed down sufficiently by the insolvency practitioner. He may find that the remaining workforce of the company has all been employed for over 20 years and that, at the time of the insolvency, all the employees had significant amounts of arrears of pay and holiday pay owing to them which had not been paid by the insolvency practitioner during the course of the receivership or administration. In this case, the purchaser could find that he has taken on a significant and unforeseen financial liability. The purchaser should certainly not expect the insolvency practitioner to inform him of this potential liability, particularly if the sale may be lost as a result. Remember – 'caveat emptor' – let the buyer beware!

Unfair dismissal

The insolvency practitioner may have dismissed employees in circumstances which could give the employees grounds for claiming unfair dismissal, although in practice such claims are rare in an insolvency. The insolvency practitioner will usually have good grounds for dismissing certain employees, for economic reasons, simply by showing that the company is insolvent. But he is under a statutory obligation to act fairly in selecting the employees to be dismissed and in their manner of dismissal.

In many insolvencies the most likely grounds for unfair treatment are:

- a failure to consult with the employee
- a failure to offer the employee available alternative employment
- unfair selection of the employee

If an employee considers that he has been unfairly dismissed, he has the right to apply to an industrial tribunal. If the tribunal finds that the complaint is justified, it may rule that the employee should be reinstated by the company. This is unlikely to be practicable in a formal insolvency so the tribunal may instead award compensation to the employee. This compensation can consist of both basic and compensatory awards which, in total, could amount to nearly £16 000.

If unfair dismissal awards are made against an insolvent company, they will rank as unsecured claims, unless the insolvency practitioner has personally adopted the employees' contracts of employment. In this case the insolvency practitioner would probably be entitled to an indemnity out of the assets of the company which are under his control. However the effects of the Litster case could mean that, in theory, this liability will be transferred to the purchaser of the business and assets of the insolvent company.

So the purchaser must ask the insolvency practitioner about the manner in which employees have been dismissed during the insolvency, in order to be satisfied that he has no potential liability for unfair dismissal.

Quantifying the potential liability

If a purchaser acquires a business as a going concern, he is likely to have a liability to the employees of the previous company. It is important for the purchaser to quantify that potential liability so that the purchase price can, if necessary, be adjusted accordingly. During the course of negotiations, the purchaser should request from the insolvency practitioner a list of all the employees as at the date of the start of the insolvency, together with the following information on each employee:

- his or her starting date with the company
- the date of dismissal (if appropriate)
- his or her age
- his or her rate of pay
- details of arrears of pay and holiday pay outstanding as at the date of the insolvency and whether or not these claims have been paid by the insolvency practitioner
- details of potential lieu of notice and redundancy claims

The insolvency practitioner may not have made the relevant calculations for lieu of notice and redundancy payments and may not feel he should do so for the purpose of the proposed sale of the business. But the other details will enable the purchaser, or his advisors, to make the necessary calculations. The purchaser can then decide whether or not the potential liability is significant and whether he should make any adjustment to the proposed purchase price.

The most significant employee liability could arise in respect of any directors of the company and the purchaser, and perhaps the insolvency practitioner, may have to negotiate with such directors in order to try to limit their potential claims. Such negotiations can often be successful if there is a chance that the purchaser will reduce his offer substantially because of the claims and that, as a result, the directors will become liable under personal guarantees.

When calculating the potential liability to employees, and any consequent reduction in the purchase price, the purchaser should attempt to be as realistic as possible. He should not simply assume that the new business will fail immediately, that the whole of the potential liability will then crystallize, and therefore that a pound-for-pound reduction in the purchase price is required. The resultant net purchase price may mean that his offer is very much lower than rival offers which have taken a more pragmatic view.

It must be remembered that the bulk of the potential liability will only become payable if, and when, the purchaser makes any of the employees he has retained redundant. Once the new business has been trading for a number of years, the difference between the actual liability of the purchaser to redundant employees and the liability as it would have been if the employees had not been transferred, may not be significant.

On the other hand, the purchaser may only want to continue the acquired business in the premises of the old company for a short period of time before transferring the business to another part of the country. In this case he may find that few of the employees will wish to go with the business and the whole of the potential liability may indeed become payable within a short time of the acquisition.

Key point summary

- The purchaser should obtain, as soon as possible, a list of all of the company's employees at the beginning of the insolvency, together with other relevant information.
- The purchaser should calculate the potential liability in respect of any employees who may be transferred to him and determine if a reduction in the purchase price is necessary.

10 What other matters should I consider?

Re-use of company's name

When a purchaser buys the shares of a company, all that changes is the ownership of the shares. Since the company appears to carry on as before, the new owners of the company may feel that a change of company name is appropriate to signify the change of ownership.

If the purchaser acquires the business and assets of a company, either before or after a formal insolvency, goodwill will usually be acquired along with the other assets. Technically, goodwill is the additional amount paid over and above the value of the physical assets. In the case of a company in trouble, the value placed on the goodwill is often a notional £1.

In *Chambers Twentieth Century Dictionary*, goodwill is defined as 'the established custom or popularity of any business or trade' and an important part of that custom is the company's name. The clause in the sale contract dealing with goodwill usually gives the purchaser the right to use any name, trade name or other trading style which had previously been used by the vendor company and to represent publicly that it is carrying on the old business.

If the business is being acquired from an insolvency practitioner, the acquisition is often carried out by means of an off-the-shelf company acquired specifically for that purpose. If the purchaser then wishes to retain the previous company's name, either the vendor company and the insolvency practitioner will agree in the contract not to object (subject to the approval of the Companies Registration Office) or the insolvency practitioner, on behalf of the vendor company, will agree to swap names. Thus in the former case, the insolvency practitioner will usually arrange to change the name of the vendor company to a suitable alternative and, in the latter, the insolvency will proceed in the name of the off-the-shelf, purchasing company with the purchasing company assuming the name of the vendor company.

There is no reason why the purchasing company should not assume exactly the same trading style as the vendor company. Indeed, it may very well carry certain benefits in terms of any continuing advertising which the vendor company may have commissioned, for example, in British Telecom's *Yellow Pages*, assuming, of course, that the purchaser retains the same address and telephone number.

In many cases though, the purchaser may wish to change the name, perhaps only in a small way, in order to try to dispel any bad feelings arising out of the insolvency. The degree of bad feeling varies tremendously from case to case. If a purchaser can clearly demonstrate that there is no connection with the vendor company, apart from the name which is being continued, the trade customers and suppliers should have few qualms about continuing their relationship with the new company. However, if members of the public have suffered in the insolvency of the vendor company, it may be more difficult to establish the required level of trust if the company's previous name is retained.

If the purchaser wishes to use the name of the previous company, he should obtain a search from Companies House to determine whether there are any other companies which are using a similar name. The existence of any such companies could affect either the value of the name or the purchaser's right to use it.

A further problem can arise from the re-use of the insolvent company's trading name if any of the directors of the previous company are re-employed by the purchaser either as directors or in any other management role. Under current insolvency legislation, this can lead to a restriction on the use of company names. The legislation states that, where a company goes into insolvent liquidation (that is, where its assets are insufficient to meet its liabilities), a director or a shadow director of that company cannot, for a period of five years from the date of the insolvency:

- be a director of any company that is known by a 'prohibited name'
- be involved in the management of such a company either directly or indirectly

The definition of a 'prohibited name' is any name by which the company in liquidation was known (either the formal name of the company or any other business or trading name) at any time during the 12 month period prior to the liquidation. The definition also covers any name which is so similar to any previous names used as to suggest an association with the company in liquidation.

A problem may arise for a purchaser of the business and assets of a company in trouble from either an administrative receiver or administrator because the purchaser will not know, at the time of the acquisition, whether the original company will eventually proceed to liquidation. It will be this subsequent liquidation which will trigger the prohibition on the re-use of the name. It must be said that companies in either administrative receivership or administration do often proceed to liquidation.

Principally, there are two ways in which the problem can be solved. In the first instance and following the liquidation of the vendor company, an application can be made to the court for the previous directors to act in whatever prohibited position is required by the purchaser. Second, in order to avoid such an application to court and where the purchasing company has acquired the business from an administrative receiver, an administrator, a liquidator or a supervisor (of a corporate voluntary arrangement), the purchaser can send a notice to all of the known creditors of the original company within 28 days of the effective purchase.

The notice to creditors should contain the following details:

- the name and registered number of the insolvent company
- the circumstances of the acquisition by the purchaser
- the otherwise prohibited name which the purchaser intends to use
- any change of the purchaser's name which will be required

It is important to note that this second alternative is not available to a purchaser of the business and assets of a company in trouble, which is not in any formal insolvency at the time of the acquisition, but which does proceed to liquidation afterwards.

The previous directors

A director of an insolvent company may face a number of problems which could include:

- disqualification from acting as a director of a company, or taking part in the management of a company, for a number of years
- a successful action for wrongful trading, resulting in having to contribute financially to the shortfall as regards the company's creditors
- personal guarantees to the company's bankers
- personal guarantees to the company's landlord in respect of any leasehold property (including a potential liability for dilapidations), or to other third parties, such as finance companies

The purchaser of the business and assets of an insolvent company will need to bear these problems in mind if he is planning to re-employ any of the directors of that company, whether or not the re-use of any trading name of the company is also being considered. Although the problems are unlikely to have any direct bearing on the purchaser, the re-employed directors may have difficulty in concentrating on their responsibilities in the new company if they fear possible litigation and financial penalties.

Much of the goodwill of the company, particularly if it is a small or medium sized company, will be personal to one or more of its directors. The purchaser should therefore give serious consideration to re-employing at least certain of the directors if he feels they are an integral part of the business. It is not always necessary to offer them a similar role in the new company. There are many occasions where previous directors are reemployed for a short period of time only, in order to smoothe the acquisition with employees and customers, and in order to extract from them the necessary understanding of the business. The same considerations may also apply to other senior employees of the previous business.

The investigation process needs to identify the likely causes of the insolvency so that the director who was perhaps its sole cause is not reemployed or, if his employment is absolutely necessary for any reason, so that enough control can be exercised over his future conduct.

Borrowing considerations

This section is principally intended for those, perhaps, inexperienced purchasers, who need to borrow a substantial part of the money required to fund the acquisition.

The importance of a corporate or individual business plan has already been discussed and nowhere is such a plan more important than when it comes to raising funds for an acquisition. The general strategy of acquisition should already have been discussed, at an early stage, with the providers of funds, be they clearing banks, venture capitalists or other lenders. The purchaser will be clear in his own mind that acquisition is the correct route forward, or perhaps one of several acceptable routes, and a likely range of available funds will already have been identified and approved.

The purchaser must prepare a specific business plan, especially if the acquisition target is a company in trouble. The purchaser cannot expect to ask his local bank manager for funding on the grounds that he has just come across a bargain company in receivership which will make his fortune in 12 months. The business plan will need to be very carefully thought out and accompanied by detailed profit and cash flow forecasts for at least a year, preferably two years and ideally, with summary forecasts for subsequent periods. It will help the purchaser if his accountants have prepared, and support, the plan and forecasts.

The plan and forecasts will show not only the initial capital required to fund the acquisition, but also the total funds required by the new venture over the forecast period. The forecasts should be prepared realistically, showing a gradual and believable improvement over a period of time rather than an overnight success (unless the latter can be clearly demonstrated!). Nothing will annoy a lender more than constant requests for further funds, together with forecasts which are never being achieved.

The banker's willingness to lend money for an acquisition will depend upon his confidence in the business of the company, whether the plans and forecasts are reasonable, and his perceived ability of, and hence his confidence in, the management. Banker's are less inclined to lend money simply on the basis of any security which may be available, be it property and debtors within the company, or guarantees from the directors. That is not to say, of course, that such security will not be required, as it surely will be.

The purchaser should appreciate that a request for funds to purchase the business of a failed company is likely to be less attractive than a request to fund a new business venture. After all, a new business venture has everything going for it, in theory at least, whereas the previous failure of a company may mean, perhaps, that the particular business just cannot succeed in that location at this time, no matter who is in the driving seat, and so the seeds of doubt are sown. The purchaser must be prepared to show clearly to the potential bankers how the new company will succeed where the previous company failed.

If the purchaser is unable to raise sufficient funds from conventional sources and before he turns to secondary sources such as remortgages or relatives' retirement funds, he should review the basic philosophy behind the desired acquisition. Buying a business from an insolvent company is very rarely the bargain which it is made out to be. There are many risks involved and there is no surer recipe for failure than an acquisition made with insufficient starting capital.

Key point summary

- If a purchaser buys a company from a receiver or an administrator and wishes to re-employ any director, he could be banned from using any name used by the old company if, and when, the old company goes into liquidation.
- The purchaser should be certain that the re-employment of any of the directors of the old company is necessary.
- The purchaser should think very carefully about the advantages and disadvantages of using an insolvent company's name before proceeding to do so.
- The potential purchaser must ensure that he has sufficient funds to make the purchase initially, and to fund future working capital.

11 Negotiating the offer

Negotiating with the previous owners

The investigation is now over and the report has been prepared. If the acquisition involves a company that is not yet in a formal insolvency, the report will include an estimate of the present balance sheet of the company (the statement of affairs), on both a going concern and a forced sale basis.

The purchaser will have made an estimate of the company's profit potential, together with an estimate of any intangible benefits which may accrue as a result of the acquisition. The purchaser will also have assessed the likely risks involved in allowing the company to proceed to a formal insolvency, and then buying the company from the insolvency practitioner. It is worth noting that there are many cases where a potential purchaser has investigated a target company which is in trouble but decided not to proceed at that time. Following a subsequent receivership or liquidation of the target company, the original purchaser has then made a successful purchase from the insolvency practitioner. The reasons are obvious; in the often competitive sale of a business from a formal insolvency, where time is usually of the essence, the purchaser best placed to make a realistic offer will be the one who has carried out an investigation prior to the insolvency.

There are several well known methods of valuing unquoted companies in general. These include return on capital employed, multiple of earnings or discounted cash flow analysis. However, where a company in trouble is being acquired, such methods are usually not applicable. The most realistic valuation will be given by the value of the net assets to be acquired by the purchaser, less an appropriate discount.

It is worth examining the statement of estimated financial position drawn up during the investigation. The statement will have identified two distinct valuations for the company; a going concern valuation which assumes that the company continues as a going concern, and a forced sale valuation where the assumption is that the business ceases and the assets are disposed of in a short period of time by way of, for example, a liquidation of the company. The purchaser should also remember that the definition of the company in trouble implies that the company is one where losses have probably been incurred over a number of years and where the company is technically, but not formally, insolvent.

We can now consider the implications of the various combinations of going concern and forced sale values which may be shown by the statement of estimated financial position.

(a) **Going concern and forced sale values both showing a total net assets position.**
It is most unlikely that many troubled companies will find themselves in this category (on the assumption that the statement has been prepared realistically by the purchaser!). The implication is that assets such as property have been undervalued on the company's previous balance sheets and that any troubles have arisen as a result of a lack of working capital so that debts cannot be paid for as and when they fall due. The company should be able to be managed the situation by having further discussions with the company's bankers, or other third parties, in order to inject further funds into the company. It is likely that remedial action will also be required to stem the company's losses.

(b) **Going concern values showing a net assets position with forced sale values showing a net liabilities position.**
Many troubled companies will find themselves in this category. In the event of a liquidation of the company (forced sale values) the creditors will not be paid in full and, thus, the first definition of insolvency (net liabilities) is satisfied and the directors may find themselves liable for wrongful trading. Moreover, a careful analysis of the current assets and liabilities will probably show that it is likely that the company cannot pay its liabilities as and when they fall due (the second definition of insolvency). The directors and shareholders are seeking a purchaser for the business as a way out of their difficulties.

(c) **Going concern and forced sale values both showing a total net liabilities position.**
The company is totally insolvent. The directors should not be talking to a potential purchaser either of the shares in the company or of the company's business and assets, but to an insolvency practitioner. The total net liabilities of the company, even on a going concern basis, means that the vendor should be paying the purchaser to take over the company; the contrary position should not be being contemplated by the purchaser. Apart from the purchase consideration, the purchaser will have to put further funds into the company in order to rectify the net liabilities position and additional funds will probably be required for working capital.

So it is assumed that the purchaser is dealing with a potential purchase where the statement of the company's financial position shows a net asset position on a going concern basis and a net liability position on a forced sale basis. Two further assumptions will also be made; first that the company cannot meet its debts as and when they fall due and thus the company is technically insolvent and, second that the vendor is dealing with only one purchaser, as is most likely to be the case in a pre-insolvency situation.

In view of the technical insolvency of the company, the purchaser should be absolutely certain that he wishes to proceed with a possible acquisition *before* a formal insolvency of the company. The combination of the price to be paid for the shares or business and assets of the company, plus the funds needed to restore the company to solvency, will invariably be greater than the price required after a formal insolvency. Two other factors may also influence the decision of the prospective purchaser: the speed with which any formal insolvency is likely to occur and the type of the insolvency.

If the troubles of the company are severe (bouncing cheques, writs, statutory demands, a winding-up petition, and so on) and the bank has requested investigating accountants to prepare a report, it will be reasonable for the purchaser to infer that a receivership is imminent and that he will not have long to wait before he can talk to a receiver about acquiring the business and assets. On the other hand, if there are none of the obvious danger signs of impending insolvency and the situation is not critical, the company could struggle on for months, or even years, before the purchaser has the opportunity to negotiate with an insolvency practitioner and the business may have been destroyed meanwhile.

The timing of a receivership appointment may also depend on the security available to the bank. If the bank is well secured on the company's freehold property or personal guarantees from the directors, it may be less inclined to appoint a receiver than if it is relying solely on debtors or stock, where the recovery or sale thereof could be used by the company to fund further losses. In the latter case the bank could see a significant reduction in its security over a period of time.

Turning to the type of insolvency, the purchaser who decides to wait for a formal insolvency may be willing to take his chances in negotiating with a receiver but, if the company's bankers do not have any floating charge security, no such appointment will be possible. In the case of a larger company, the directors would have the ability to request the court to appoint an administrator who, again, the purchaser may be happy to deal with. But in the small or medium sized company, such an appointment is unlikely, for the reasons given in Chapter 3, and the purchaser will find that he is left to deal with a liquidator and the likelihood that little remains of the company's business.

Share purchase or business and assets

Once the purchaser has decided that he does want to negotiate with the original owners of the company, he has two options: a purchase of the company's shares or a purchase of the business and assets only.

If the statement of estimated financial position shows that the forced sale deficiency is very large with only a small estimated surplus arising on a going concern basis, the purchaser should only consider a purchase of the business and assets of the company. If the shares were acquired, the additional amount required to restore the company to solvency would be great and, meanwhile, the purchaser would be taking on all the risks associated with an insolvent company (wrongful trading, possible disqualification of directors, and so on) if, for whatever reason, the company under the new ownership did not succeed.

If the statement of the company's financial position shows a large potential surplus on a going concern basis and only a small deficiency on a forced sale basis, both options remain open. In such a case the purchaser should not forget that, in order to be covered by the definition of a company in trouble, the company is still suffering from significant difficulties and that its principal problem is likely to be that it has large arrears of creditors. If the purchaser is considering a share purchase, he will have to take the following factors into account:

- the likely purchase price of the company's shares
- the amount required to restore the company to solvency (paying arrears of creditors and additional working capital)
- the extent of the company's problems and the ability of the purchaser to eliminate those problems; that is, the risk of the company not succeeding after the acquisition
- the strength of any warranties which will be included in the sale agreement

When negotiating the price, the purchaser should be aware that he is likely to have the upper hand. He is probably the only purchaser that the vendors are dealing with and, if the sale does not go ahead, their only alternative will be a formal insolvency.

There is no magic formula for setting the right price to pay for the shares of the company. The statement of financial position will give an indication of the value of the shares but the purchaser will also have to take account of all the other factors which were discussed earlier in this book.

Once the purchaser has established a price which he is prepared to offer for the shares, he should not be persuaded to increase it. The company's troubles are such that the price is likely to be insignificant and there will be little scope, or time, for negotiation. If the offer is not accepted, the purchaser should walk away from the deal, perhaps to negotiate shortly with an insolvency practitioner.

There will be more scope for negotiation if the purchaser is considering the acquisition of only the business and assets of the company. However, because the vendor company will probably proceed to liquidation after the sale is concluded, as discussed in Chapter 4, the purchaser must ensure that a fair price is paid for the business and assets if he is to avoid a possible attack on the transaction by a liquidator. There will be less risk of attack if the price is based upon the going concern valuation, because it is a going concern which is being acquired.

In view of the risks that the purchaser is taking when acquiring a technically insolvent company prior to a formal insolvency, he must obtain adequate professional advice throughout the investigation and negotiation process. This advice should be obtained from insolvency specialists in both the accounting and legal professions.

The purchaser will invariably be advised not to proceed with any pre-insolvency acquisition of a company in trouble because there will be too little time in which to carry out an adequate investigation. Even in the few cases where this is possible, the purchaser will probably be advised that the potential cost of, and the risks involved in, the acquisition will be too great. Instead it will be suggested to the purchaser that he waits to negotiate with the receiver. This subject is dealt with next.

Negotiating with the insolvency practitioner

The insolvency practitioner has three ways of disposing of the business and assets of the insolvent company:

- by auction
- by private treaty
- by tender sale

An auction is rarely used for the sale of a business. It is more appropriately used for the sale of assets only and, consequently, it is the method most used when assets are being sold out of a liquidation for example. Similarly a private treaty sale is rarely used by receivers and administrators. It restricts the insolvency practitioner to negotiating with only one potential purchaser and so may not achieve the full market price for the business because the market will not have been adequately tested. In addition such negotiations can be very protracted as there is no incentive for the purchaser to act quickly. The sale of the business and assets by tender is most frequently used where a going concern sale is desired.

The purchaser should note that a formal tender procedure is rarely used, with all potential purchasers having but one attempt at making an offer. Rather the process is informal and, provided the initial offer is within a broad range of acceptable values, the purchasers will get further opportunities to increase their offers.

The insolvency practitioner will hold asset valuations, usually obtained from professional valuers, and will have compiled his own statement of affairs. In his own mind, the insolvency practitioner will expect to dispose of the business and assets at a value somewhere between the going concern and forced sale values. But because his duty is to obtain the best possible price for the assets of the company for the benefit of the company's creditors, he is unlikely to divulge any valuation which he has obtained or, indeed, any guide price whatsoever for the assets which he is attempting to dispose of. There have been situations where an eventual disposal of assets has taken place at a price in excess of the estimated going concern value, although it must be said that such cases usually result, in the end, in the only source of repeat business for insolvency practitioners.

The insolvency practitioner may publicise the availability of the business and assets in a variety of ways including:

- advertisements on the local and national press
- advertisements in trade magazines
- specific mail shots or telephone calls to known interested parties
- general mail shots to specific categories of potential purchasers (obtained from *Yellow Pages* for example)

The advertising is considered to be essential so that the insolvency practitioner can demonstrate that the business has been fully exposed to the market place and, therefore, that the price which is eventually obtained by him is the best which could have been achieved in the circumstances. The first advertisement will probably be placed in the *Financial Times*, if the size of the business warrants the costs involved, on the Tuesday following the date of the appointment. Advertisements in other appropriate newspapers or trade magazines will follow as soon as possible thereafter. In practice, most insolvency practitioners would probably agree that the eventual purchaser is unlikely to be found as a result of this general advertising but rather from mail shots to people who are known to have an interest in the business or from people who hear about the availability of the business on the grapevine.

Following the advertising of the sale of the business, the insolvency practitioner will send out further details of the assets available for sale to all people who express an interest. This sales pack will normally contain the following information:

- a brief history of the company
- details of the company's business and its products or services
- company sales literature
- summary details of the assets which are available for sale (including detailed lists if not too cumbersome)
- employee details, usually in summary form
- extracts from the company's accounts, usually including the latest set of audited accounts

Prospective purchasers will then have some time to view the assets and make any enquiries they deem to be necessary. The length of this period will vary from insolvency to insolvency; a simple, clean disposal of assets with many interested purchasers would probably lead to a relatively short investigation period, perhaps of only ten working days or so. Alternatively, the sale of a larger business, particularly with only a few potential purchasers, may lead to an investigation period of several weeks or more.

During the investigation period, when the purchaser may well be having discussions with the company's employees, it could be worthwhile for the purchaser to try to establish a good relationship with one or more of the company's management team. The purchaser may then be able to obtain feedback about other parties who are also interested in the acquisition. The insolvency practitioner needs to obtain the best possible price for the business and assets of the company and this can most easily be achieved by having several interested parties bidding against each other. If the purchaser can find out who the other interested parties are, he may be in a position to gauge their level of interest and thus the price that they will be willing to pay.

The purchaser should understand the priorities of the insolvency practitioner. In a group situation for example, the insolvency practitioner may be dealing with potential purchasers who are interested in the whole group and he may be less interested in dealing with purchasers who are only interested in individual companies. He is likely to continue discussions with such purchasers though in order to keep all his options open. In the end he will want to pursue the course of action which is going to achieve the best realisations for the group as a whole.

Similarly the insolvency practitioner may be less interested in dealing with a purchaser who is interested in acquiring only part of the business and assets of a company than with a purchaser who is prepared to take the whole of the business. To use an auction analogy, if all of the assets of a company in liquidation were to be auctioned, the better assets would be likely to attract a large number of buyers who will force up the realisable value of all assets but, in particular, the less important assets. This may not be the case if the better assets are disposed of prior to the auction, albeit for a good price, and the remaining assets achieve very little on the subsequent auction.

The purchaser may find it useful to have the services of an insolvency specialist on his negotiating team since he will best understand the insolvency practitioner's priorities. Whether such a person should take a visible role in the negotiations will depend upon the individual circumstances and the advice of the insolvency specialist. In certain cases the insolvency practitioner conducting the sale may be antagonised if the purchaser's specialist has an active and visible role in the proceedings.

If the insolvency practitioner is continuing the business to dispose of it as a going concern, the length of the investigation period will be a trade-off between the usually high costs of continuing to trade, perhaps at a loss, and the chances of obtaining better realisations for the assets. If no prospective purchaser is found or if the offers received are less than the forced sale valuations which have been obtained by the insolvency practitioner, he will eventually cease trading and dispose of the assets piecemeal, by auction for example.

The prospective purchaser should note that the longer the insolvency practitioner continues to trade, the more he is likely to accept a reduced price for the sale of the business and assets, always provided that the sale price exceeds the break-up or forced sale valuations that he has obtained. Of course for the purchaser, the dilemma is that the longer it takes after the formal insolvency for the sale to be completed, the less of a business he is likely to acquire, with more associated problems such as the departure of key staff, the loss of customers, problems with suppliers and so on.

Following the investigation period, the insolvency practitioner will usually write to all parties who have expressed an interest in the business, requesting them to make offers for the business and assets. Following the initial discussions with potential purchasers, he may well specify the particular assets or parts of the business for which offers should be made. This is done in order to try to make the various offers compatible with each other so that the highest offer can easily be established.

It is possible that offers for at least certain of the assets may be requested not in absolute financial terms but by reference to a formula. For example, it would be usual to make an offer for stock and work in progress 'at valuation' or 'at cost less a percentage'. The actual value of the stock will then be computed at the date of completion by reference to the formula.

After the initial round of offers, the insolvency practitioner may well accept the highest offer there and then. More likely, the insolvency practitioner will realise that the offers that he has received are simply opening bids, with purchasers attempting to buy the business at an unrealistically low price. He is therefore likely to select the highest three or four offers and either negotiate with each of them in order to increase the offers or, in a relatively straightforward case, he may just issue a further deadline and request 'best and final' offers by that time and date.

During final negotiations with several potential purchasers, the so-called 'Dutch' auction may arise, with purchasers effectively bidding against each other. Neither the insolvency practitioner nor the prospective purchasers are likely to relish this but, if purchasers have been underbidding and have not yet reached their maximum purchase price, it is often unavoidable. A bidder will telephone the insolvency practitioner soon after the deadline has expired in order to see if his offer has been successful. He will be told that he has not been successful and he will then ask something to the effect of 'What if I were to increase my offer by £10 000?'. The insolvency practitioner will then be placed in a difficult position but he is still under an obligation to obtain the best possible price for the assets, and so a Dutch auction begins.

For the subsequent negotiations to proceed smoothly, the purchaser will have to decide at this stage whether there are certain basic conditions that he is going to insist upon including in the subsequent contract. Any such conditions must be discussed, at least in principal, with the insolvency practitioner so that the purchaser can be sure that such matters can eventually be resolved. If the discussions reveal fundamental problems or differences of opinion that will never be compromised by the insolvency practitioner, the purchaser should walk away from the acquisition at this stage rather than incur further time and expense.

When a bid has finally been accepted, a further period of discussion may well follow in order to establish the basic 'heads of agreement' prior to detailed negotiations over the contract. All discussions up to this stage will have been 'subject to contract'. The final part of the negotiations will involve a discussion between the various parties, including solicitors for each side, to finalise the contract. Some of the features peculiar to sales contracts from insolvency practitioners are discussed in the next chapter. If the purchaser has carried out a proper investigation and taken adequate professional advice during the previous stages, there should be no need for any further discussions about the price which has already been agreed between the purchaser and the insolvency practitioner.

It is usually only if proper advice has not been obtained by the purchaser that the contract meeting will turn into a long, and probably heated, affair. If the purchaser, at this late stage, tries to reduce the agreed price because of an unforeseen problem, the insolvency practitioner may well withdraw from further discussions and revert to an alternative purchaser. There will invariably be other purchasers that the insolvency practitioner is keeping in reserve.

The period between the acceptance of the offer by the insolvency practitioner and the contract meeting is likely to be short, often only one or two days. The insolvency practitioner will have instructed his solicitors to prepare a basic contract shortly after his appointment, as soon as he is aware of the likely format of the sale. Consequently the purchaser must ensure at an early stage that he has sufficient funds in place to proceed quickly.

During the negotiation process, the purchaser or his solicitor may become frustrated by the receiver's apparent lack of concern or enthusiasm; telephone calls may not be returned promptly, faxes may not be answered and the receiver may not be available if the purchaser turns up at his offices or at the insolvent company's premises. The purchaser must remember that the insolvency practitioner may be dealing with a number of sales at the same time and, although of extreme importance to the purchaser, the particular sale may be less important to the insolvency practitioner. It is in such circumstances that the purchaser may enjoy a further benefit of having a local insolvency specialist or solicitor on his acquisition team: to put it simply, strings can be pulled.

In addition the purchaser should establish the identity of the person within the insolvency practitioner's practice who is actually responsible for the conclusion of the sale. With larger sales or in smaller practices this will probably be the insolvency practitioner himself. With smaller sales or in larger practices the insolvency practitioner will probably delegate the negotiations to an experienced senior manager or manager.

During the final negotiations or as a condition of the final offer, the purchaser may be asked to give a deposit in respect of the proposed purchase. The deposit will either be in addition to, or may be substituted for, the normal deposit which becomes payable on the legal exchange of contracts. The beneficiary of the interest on the deposit is a matter for negotiation between the parties.

The purpose of the deposit is as follows:

- to ensure that the purchaser is serious and not merely wasting time
- to give an indication as to the financial worth of the purchaser
- to assist in a speedy conclusion of the transaction

Instead of a deposit but for the same reasons, the purchaser will usually be required to supply bank or similar references to show that he has the required funds available for the proposed purchase or that he will have access to sufficient funds at the time of the proposed completion. If funding is delayed, the insolvency practitioner will invariably turn to an alternative purchaser.

One further point should be stressed. All negotiations are subject to contract and the insolvency practitioner is under an obligation to obtain the best possible price for the assets of the company. Consequently the insolvency practitioner will still be at liberty to accept a better offer from another purchaser at any point in time after a deal has been agreed, prior to exchange of contracts.

In practice the insolvency practitioner is unlikely to start fresh negotiations with a new purchaser once existing negotiations have reached an advanced stage, unless the offer from the new purchaser is significantly greater than the existing offer. To do so may incur additional costs which may exceed the difference in price between the two offers. The insolvency practitioner also takes the risk of losing both interested parties. In order to minimise the risk of a better offer being accepted, the purchaser must be prepared to complete the whole negotiation process quickly.

Occasionally a purchaser will make an offer to the insolvency practitioner which must be accepted 'within 24 hours' or similar, otherwise the offer will be withdrawn. The deadline is usually set for some time prior to that set by the insolvency practitioner for the receipt of offers. This tactic rarely works: if the purchaser is making a high offer, the insolvency practitioner may be able to accept it after taking advice from his agents and after reviewing the progress of the negotiations with other interested parties. However the purchaser is usually trying to force the insolvency practitioner into accepting a very low offer which simply cannot be accepted without fully testing the market. If the purchaser is genuinely interested in the business and assets and chooses to adopt this tactic, he may only alienate the insolvency practitioner as a result.

Although the insolvency practitioner must obtain the best possible price for the assets, he may not simply accept the highest price which is offered to him. For example, he may feel that the highest bidder will not be able to complete the purchase and, rather than risk losing all other potential purchasers, he may accept a lower but more financially sound offer in the first place. There are various other reasons as to why an insolvency practitioner may not take the highest offer received, suffice to say that he would have to be able to justify his decision if called upon to do so.

The tactics of the final bid will depend upon the degree of face-to-face negotiation, the skills of the negotiating team (on both sides) and any knowledge of the competition.

In a simple situation, the amount of negotiation is likely to be minimal and there is an argument that the purchaser should simply put forward his best offer at the beginning of the negotiation process; if the offer is successful, all will be well, otherwise the purchaser should put the affair down to experience and move on to the next acquisition.

Key point summary

- If the purchaser is considering the acquisition of a company in trouble prior to a formal insolvency, he should be absolutely certain that he is fully aware of the risks involved and the likely cost of the acquisition, including any 'hidden' costs.
- The purchaser should be prepared to act very quickly in carrying out the negotiations, particularly after a formal insolvency.
- The purchaser should establish the maximum price which he is willing to pay and should not be persuaded to increase this.
- The longer the insolvency practitioner has been trading the business, the lower the price he will be prepared to accept.
- The longer the insolvency practitioner has been trading the business, the less of a business may be available to the purchaser.
- The negotiations will be subject to contract and a deal is never concluded, especially with an insolvency practitioner, until the contract is signed.

12   Should I sign the contract?

This chapter identifies some of the specific features which are peculiar to contracts with insolvency practitioners. It is not intended to provide potential purchasers with a ready made precedent that they can then compare with the contract that they have received from the insolvency practitioner's solicitors. Purchasers should always obtain their own legal advice when making any acquisition, especially when buying a company in trouble.

In the purchase of a business outside an insolvency, the contract is usually drawn up by the purchaser's solicitors with the interests of the purchaser very much in mind. Where a business is being acquired as a going concern from an insolvency practitioner, the contract will be drawn up by the practitioner's solicitors. The contract may be somewhat shorter than expected, because it will not include many of the usual clauses and warranties which are present in a sale agreement for a solvent company.

The parties to the contract

In a sale of the business and assets of a company by an insolvency practitioner, the usual parties to the contract are:

- the original insolvent company (the vendor)
- the insolvency practitioner (often two are appointed)
- the purchaser
- any guarantors

One of the principal parties to the contract will be the original company, notwithstanding the fact that it is formally insolvent, and it is the company which will be selling its business and assets to the purchaser. Since the original company is insolvent, it is important to note that any claim by the purchaser against the vendor, for breach of contract for example, may be worthless. After the costs of the insolvency and the distribution of funds to the debenture holder, there may be little or no funds available against which the purchaser could make a claim. Even if funds are available, the purchaser's claim is likely to be unsecured, and will therefore rank alongside the claims of the other unsecured creditors of the company, and after the claims of the preferential creditors.

Similarly, the insolvency practitioner is usually only a party to the contract as agent for the original company and as a means of getting the original, insolvent company to execute the sale contract. Unless any breach of duty or other such claim can be brought against the insolvency practitioner personally, a claim for breach of contract against the insolvency practitioner will be a claim against the original company by virtue of the agency.

The purchaser should obviously ensure that the correct vendor companies are included in the sale contract. The physical presence of an asset on the company's premises need not necessarily mean that the asset belongs to that company. In a group situation, individual group companies often have responsibility for certain specific functions within the group, such as the holding of all group properties or dealing with all group vehicles. After manufacture by one company, stock may be transferred to another group company for subsequent sale outside the group, even though the stock may not move physically on the intra-group transfer. Similarly a particular asset which is physically on the premises of one company may have been loaned from another group company.

The directors and shareholders of the original company are not party to the contract and it is usually not possible for the purchaser to insist that the original directors or shareholders enter into any restrictive trading agreement, as would usually be the case in an agreement for the sale of shares in a solvent company, for example. Such a clause would try to prohibit the original shareholders from carrying on the same business as the company in a certain area for a specified time.

If the potential purchaser of the business genuinely believes that competition from any previous shareholders or directors may jeopardise the purchase of the business, it may be possible for the purchaser to enter into a separate agreement with them, provided that the insolvency practitioner knows where they can be found and can persuade them to do so. It is also possible that the insolvency practitioner could take action against the previous directors (usually at the expense of the purchaser) if it can be proved that they have acquired any part of the business or trade of the previous company for no consideration. Alternatively, the purchaser may well consider reemploying certain of the previous directors or shareholders, at least for a short period of time, thus creating a contractual relationship between them and the purchaser.

Validity of appointment

The appointed insolvency practitioner is an important party to the sale agreement, even though he will usually only be acting as agent for the vendor. Since the insolvency practitioner is conducting the sale, it is vital for the purchaser to ensure that the insolvency practitioner is authorised to deal with the assets which are being sold. If the insolvency practitioner has not been validly appointed, he will not have the ability or authority to deal with the assets.

In the case of an administrative receivership, the purchaser's solicitors will require copies of the following documents:

- the deed of appointment
- evidence that the appointment has been validly accepted by the administrative receivers
- the debenture
- the letter of demand from the debenture holder

If he has not already done so, the purchaser should obtain a copy of the company search (from Companies House) which will give evidence of the registration of the debenture, the company's memorandum and articles of association, the register of charges, details of the company's directors and other useful information.

The purchaser's solicitors will then be able to check that the appointment of the receivers meets the legal requirements, including ascertaining that:

- both receivers should have accepted their appointments before the end of the business day following the day on which they received their appointment document
- both receivers should have confirmed their appointment in writing within seven days
- the debenture and the appointment should enable the receivers to act jointly and severally
- the debenture should have been registered within 21 days of its creation
- the debenture should have been correctly executed
- the demand for repayment from the debenture holder should have been validly made

The purchaser's solicitors may consider that it is necessary to try to obtain a warranty from the receivers that they have been validly appointed.

In the case of an administration, the purchaser should request a copy of the administration order from the administrator, together with copies of any other orders which may have been made by the court following his appointment. The purchaser's solicitors should also check to see whether or not the administrator's proposals have been agreed by a meeting of the company's creditors.

Guarantors

In a purchase of a business as a going concern, the purchase is often undertaken either by an off-the-shelf company which has been acquired by the purchaser's solicitors specifically for that purpose, or by an existing but usually dormant subsidiary already belonging to the purchaser. After the purchase, the assets acquired by the company will be matched by equal and opposite liabilities in the form of either an inter-company loan account (from the parent company) or by bank borrowings, which have been used to fund the acquisition of the business and assets. Thus, it is likely that the purchasing company will have little net value at this stage.

The sale contract may include several post-contractual obligations on the part of the purchaser and, because of the initial financial standing of the purchasing company, it is usual for these obligations to be guaranteed by one or more third parties. Indeed, the insolvency practitioner is not to know that the purchasing company will not also become insolvent, and sooner rather than later. The existence of guarantors in the contract means that all the purchaser's obligations will be fulfilled.

Normally the guarantor will be the holding company or other financially sound associate of the purchasing company. In certain cases, it may be appropriate to have a different company as guarantor or, indeed, the directors of, or other individuals connected with, the purchasing company, particularly where the shareholders of the purchasing company are individuals and are not involved with any other company.

Which assets are being sold?

The sale agreement will disclose the various categories of asset which the purchaser intends to acquire including:

- goodwill
- freehold or leasehold property
- plant, machinery, office equipment and motor vehicles
- stock and work in progress
- the benefit of any contracts or agreements

In its simplest form, the contract will state that the assets being sold are all those assets which fall into the defined categories of assets, which are owned by the vendor company at completion and which are situated at the company's premises at that date.

The sale agreement will usually state that the vendor company is only giving 'such right, title and interest' as it may have in the assets which are being sold. Thus, the vendor company (and the insolvency practitioner) is giving no assurance or guarantee that the assets being sold are actually owned by the vendor company. Those assets which are definitely known to belong to third parties will usually be specifically excluded from the contract and, similarly, assets subject to hire purchase, leasing or other finance contracts may also specifically be excluded.

The insolvency practitioner may not even be able to guarantee the whereabouts of all of the company's assets, particularly if the company's books and records are not up to date. This may have particular relevance, for example, if the assets in question consist of scaffolding, vehicles or plant on hire to customers, or perhaps where there are a large number of retail outlets.

The clauses dealing with the sale of the assets are normally couched in general terms because the insolvency practitioner may not be certain of the precise ownership of the assets. He will only have had charge of the company for a comparatively short period of time and the directors of the company may not be giving their full cooperation or may have been dismissed and no longer be available.

It is usually possible for the purchaser to have appended to the contract, or disclosed in a side letter, a list of assets which are being sold and a list of assets which are excluded, which belong to third parties or which are subject to finance agreements, for example. However, the insolvency practitioner would rarely be willing to state that such lists were definitive. If a detailed list of available assets was included in the contract, there would usually be further clauses in the contract to say that:

- no warranties are given that such a list is complete
- the list is only correct to the best of the knowledge and belief of both the vendor and the insolvency practitioner
- if any asset is found to be missing from such a list, the purchaser will not be entitled to any refund, proportional or otherwise, of the purchase price

It is up to the purchaser to ensure that he is fully aware of the assets which are being acquired and he may want to make a physical inspection of the assets at, or immediately before, completion, in order to obtain the required level of comfort. Alternatively, the value of the chattel assets being acquired may be insignificant when compared with the total consideration, including the property and other assets, and the purchaser can therefore afford to take a commercial risk. If significant assets are being acquired, particularly specialised plant, the purchaser must take further steps to prove to himself that the assets exist and are validly owned by the vendor company.

These terms may appear formidable as far as the purchaser is concerned but the fact remains that purchasers do complete sale agreements because of the commercial situation which exists and the overall price which is being paid for the assets. The purchaser will also have obtained a large degree of comfort during the course of the investigation and from other enquiries that he has made.

In most sale agreements by insolvency practitioners, the following assets will be stated as being specifically excluded from the sale:

- cash in hand and at bank
- any book debts due to either the vendor company or the insolvency practitioner
- any assets in the possession of, but not owned by, the vendor company
- any assets subject to finance agreements
- any claims (such as insurance claims or claims for repayment of tax) made by the vendor company or the insolvency practitioner prior to completion

The exclusion of items not owned by the vendor company will extend to stock and other assets which may be subject to reservation of title claims and this subject has been dealt with separately in Chapter 8.

The purchaser's solicitors will need to obtain a release from the debenture holder who has appointed the receiver, in respect of all assets which are being acquired. The speed at which the sale is usually concluded means this is often dealt with by way of an undertaking from the receiver's solicitors. The purchaser's solicitors will also need to ensure that the interests of any other charge holder will be handled satisfactorily by the receiver, or his solicitors. The register of charges will show other possible charge holders although, in many cases, old charges may have been satisfied some time ago and the register simply not updated.

In an administration, the administrator can freely sell assets subject to a floating charge. He may also be trying to sell a variety of charged assets such as:

- freehold or leasehold property
- assets subject to hire purchase or leasing agreements
- assets subject to reservation of title claims

The administrator may have obtained the court's agreement to the sale of such assets, in which case a copy of the relevant court order should be obtained. Otherwise the purchaser should try to obtain the agreement of the holders of any charges that the assets in question can indeed be sold by the administrator.

The sale agreement is usually concluded very speedily. Consequently, it will normally provide that any assets which are not being acquired by the purchaser, for example, any assets which are subject to finance agreements which are not being taken over by the purchaser, can remain on the company's premises for a period of time pending either their disposal by the insolvency practitioner or their collection by the appropriate finance companies. The purchaser will also, usually, be required to undertake not to use such assets until they are removed.

Caveat emptor

The sale agreement will usually contain several clauses which will attempt to limit any liability on the part of both the vendor company and, more particularly, the insolvency practitioner. In the case of the insolvency practitioner, one of the main purposes of such clauses is to ensure that the sale is clean and tidy such that there are no remaining potential liabilities which could cause him concern in the future. As soon as the sale is concluded he will want to do whatever else is necessary to conclude his appointment, as soon as possible, so that he can give his full attention to the next appointment. Examples of such clauses are:

(a) The purchaser will have to agree that, with regard to the assets which are being acquired and to the state, quality and condition of those assets, he is relying absolutely on both his own opinion and on the opinion of those professional advisors who may be assisting him.
(b) The purchaser will have to acknowledge that he has had an opportunity both to inspect fully the assets being sold and to make any necessary enquiries about those assets, and that he is fully aware of the need to rely on such an opportunity because of the absence of any warranties.

(c) The purchaser will have to agree that he has not relied on any verbal or written statement from the vendor company, the insolvency practitioner or any agents or staff employed by them, other than that which is actually written into the sale contract, and that the knowledge of such persons about the business is necessarily limited.

(d) The purchaser will have to acknowledge that he has made all the necessary enquiries about what is being purchased under, and all other matters contained in, the sale agreement.

(e) The purchaser will have to acknowledge that the conditions contained in the sale agreement are reasonable in the context of a sale by an insolvent company and that, if the sale was being made by any other than an insolvent company, a higher price would have been paid.

(f) The purchaser will have to acknowledge that the insolvency practitioner is only acting as an agent of the vendor company and will incur no personal liability whatsoever.

The purchaser will have to accept that, apart from any rare examples which may have to be given, there will be no warranties contained in the sale agreement, from either the vendor company or the insolvency practitioner. At best, the insolvency practitioner may be prepared to warrant that he has not done anything which would mean that the vendor company cannot sell what is being sold under the sale agreement.

Again, all these matters appear to be very biased in favour of the vendor company and the insolvency practitioner but they do form the basis on which sales by insolvency practitioners are usually made. The clauses in any particular sale agreement will depend upon the negotiations which have taken place between the purchaser and the insolvency practitioner. Potential purchasers should be aware that it is only in very exceptional cases that clauses such as those stated, or derivatives thereof, are omitted from sale agreements.

Property

The sale of any freehold or leasehold properties may be addressed either in the main sale contract or in a supplementary contract and it is the sale of such properties which may lead to delays in the signing of the principal contract. Obviously, the acquisition of any properties is likely to form the principal part of the total consideration paid in any particular case and the purchaser, and especially his solicitors, will want to be certain that any purchase of such properties is both safe and secure.

As with other assets, the purchaser will not be able to obtain any warranties from the vendor company with regard to any freehold or leasehold properties. The purchaser's solicitors should therefore make full enquiries, in respect of each property, with regard to:

● the title to the property
● all local land charges

- any notices served by, or other matters relating to, any local, public or other authority
- any planning legislation
- all matters revealed by any search of any authority, or which might be revealed by any such search

If the agreement involves the purchase of leasehold property, it will probably be necessary to obtain the consent of the landlord in order for the lease to be assigned to the purchaser. In many cases this consent cannot be obtained in the usually short period of time prior to exchange of contracts. The lease will usually contain a clause to the effect that the landlord's consent to an assignment cannot be unreasonably withheld and the purchaser will need to examine the lease carefully for such a clause and for any other clauses which may affect an assignment. He must be certain that the assignment can, ultimately, proceed. The purchaser will have to pay particular attention to any lease which contains a clause to the effect that the lease is automatically forfeited on the appointment of an insolvency practitioner to the lessee company.

Pending the formal assignment, which can take a considerable period of time, the purchaser can usually be granted a licence to occupy the premises, provided that he becomes responsible for all the expenses in connection with the property, and provided he exchanges contracts for the purchase of the property.

The consideration

The negotiations with the insolvency practitioner will resolve the apportionment of the total consideration between the various categories of assets being acquired. The total consideration, less any deposit which may have been paid by the purchaser, will be payable in full on completion. In view of the fact that even the most reputable purchasers have been known to stop a cheque after purchase, payment is usually made by means of a bankers' draft, usually drawn on a London clearing bank.

If completion involves a stock take, the formula for agreeing the value of the stock take will stipulate that payment must be made shortly after the stock take has been completed. The purchaser may even be required to make a payment on account of such stock on completion of the sale contract itself, with a balancing amount paid by, or refunded to, the purchaser after the stock valuation is completed.

It is rare for the insolvency practitioner to agree to defer any part of the purchase price. Where, in exceptional circumstances, this is agreed to, the purchaser will have to pay a deposit on completion that is equal to, or better than, the forced sale value of the assets which are being acquired. In addition, the insolvency practitioner will inevitably require both a charge over the purchasing company and an agreement from the purchaser that the title in all of the assets which are being acquired will not pass to the purchaser until the full consideration has been paid. The insolvency practitioner will want to protect himself from a potential default on the deferred element of the price by demanding a degree of security greatly in excess of the amount of the deferred consideration. This will severely restrict the level of security which the purchaser can offer to any bank which may be funding the purchase.

Value Added Tax

In normal circumstances, when a VAT registered company disposes of fixed assets, stock or goodwill, the disposal is treated as a taxable supply and VAT must be charged on the transaction. Where a business is transferred or sold as a going concern then, subject to certain conditions being met, the transaction will not be regarded as a taxable supply and the transaction will, effectively, be treated as being outside the scope of VAT.

For a transaction to be treated as a transfer of a going concern, the following conditions must be met:

- the business must be a going concern at the time of the sale or transfer and there must be no significant break in the usual trade of the business either before or after the transfer
- the purchaser must either be registered for VAT or become registered for VAT at the time of the transfer
- the purchaser must be able to carry on a business with the assets which are being transferred and the purchaser must be intending to use the assets acquired to carry on the same kind of business as was previously carried on by the original company

In many cases, the sale of the business and assets of an insolvent company by an insolvency practitioner will be assumed to be a sale of a going concern and the contract will contain a clause stating that the purchaser undertakes to pay any VAT associated with the sale, only if the authorities should rule that the transfer is not a sale of a going concern. As an alternative, it may be possible to obtain a written ruling from Customs and Excise as to the correct treatment of the sale, although time constraints may serve to rule out this possibility.

It is very important for the purchaser to establish the correct VAT status of the transaction. If VAT is charged on a transaction and paid by the purchaser, and it is subsequently discovered that VAT should not have been charged, then the VAT which would be reclaimed by the purchaser as input tax may be disallowed. Obviously, the amount involved could be significant and the purchaser may only be left with a claim against an insolvent vendor.

Books and records

Ownership of the accounting books and other records of the vendor company will remain with that company although certain records, such a list of the company's customers or suppliers, may be included in the sale agreement. Where the purchaser takes over the property of the vendor company, the sale agreement usually specifies that the books and records of the company may be stored on the premises for a period of time (usually, free of charge) or until the vendor company goes into liquidation, when they will become the responsibility of the liquidator.

The agreement will also allow the insolvency practitioner or his staff access to the records for a period of time and, perhaps, the use of a room for the duration.

Other matters

- **Press statements:** a clause is usually inserted into the contract stating that both the purchaser and the insolvency practitioner should mutually agree to any press statement to be issued by either party in connection with the sale.
- **Employees:** the purchaser should ensure that, as far as possible, the question of the employees of the vendor company is covered adequately by the sale contract. This subject is covered more fully in Chapter 9.
- **Post-completion matters:** if the purchaser wishes, it is normal practice for the vendor company and the insolvency practitioner to agree in the sale contract to do whatever else that is necessary for the purchaser to complete the acquisition of the business and assets. This may include the novation of any contracts or the assignment of any finance agreements, for example. The purchaser is usually required to bear any resultant costs incurred by the vendor company or the insolvency practitioner.
- **Indemnity for costs:** if the purchaser does anything after completion in relation to the sale of the business which results in costs being incurred by the vendor company or the insolvency practitioner, the purchaser will have to give an indemnity in respect of such costs.
- **Confidentiality:** purchasers of businesses in general often require a clause to be inserted in the sale agreement whereby the parties agree to keep the contents of the sale agreement confidential, and in particular, the price paid for the business and assets, unless any such disclosure is required by law. Unfortunately, it is a legal requirement of all the corporate insolvency procedures that information about receipts and payments becomes a matter of public knowledge within a short period of time. Such details must be placed on the company's file at the Companies Registration Office on a regular basis where they are open to inspection by any member of the public.

Completion

As already stated, sale agreements with insolvency practitioners are usually concluded speedily. It is normally in the interests of both the insolvency practitioner and the purchaser to complete the actual transfer of the business as soon as possible and, in many cases the signing, exchange and completion of the contract take place simultaneously.

A delay of up to a month may occur where freehold or leasehold property is involved. However, it should still be possible for the sale of the remaining assets and business to be completed earlier, on exchange, with the purchaser being granted a licence to occupy the premises until the property sale is also completed. In such an instance, the contract for the sale of the property or properties would usually be exchanged at the same time as the exchange and completion of the main sale contract.

Key point summary

- The purchaser must employ solicitors, preferably with insolvency experience, to advise on the sale contract which will be drawn up by the insolvency practitioner's solicitors.
- Initially, the purchaser's solicitors must check that the insolvency practitioner has been validly appointed.
- The purchaser is responsible for checking the existence and nature of the assets being acquired.
- The purchaser should not expect to receive any warranties whatsoever from the insolvency practitioner.
- The purchaser, and his solicitors, must be prepared to act quickly.

13   The aftermath

Specific problems

The acquisition is now complete but a number of other items need to be sorted out as quickly as possible. Some of these details may seem trifling, but overlooking them can all too often lead to embarrassing situations.

Although the purchaser is acquiring an existing business, the new owner of that business, the purchasing company, is likely to be a new legal entity. The purchaser's accountants should be able to advise on the various statutory matters that need sorting out. This includes registering the new company with Customs and Excise for VAT purposes (which may have been done already to take advantage of the VAT exemption on the purchase of the business and assets) and with the Inspector of Taxes to set up a new employee PAYE scheme. The purchaser must also remember to collect from the vendor (or the insolvency practitioner) all the necessary documentation relating to the employees.

The purchaser should not overlook the question of stationery. If the business has been acquired from an insolvency practitioner, the acquisition will probably have taken place quickly. All the existing stationery is usually removed on completion of the contract and subsequently destroyed. This will apply even if the purchaser intends to use the same name as the previous company. So entirely new stationery will be required, which must conform to the requirements of the Companies Acts.

Following the sale of the business, the insolvency practitioner will probably still be dealing with the debtors and creditors of the vendor company. Unless alternative arrangements have been made, the insolvency practitioner will probably have arranged for all post relating to the vendor company to be redirected to his office address. The Post Office redirects according to the company name specified in the redirection order. If the purchaser is trading under a completely different name from the vendor company, this should not present a problem. However, if the purchaser is intending to use the same, or a similar, name as the vendor company, then he will need to make forwarding arrangements with the insolvency practitioner.

The vendor will ensure that final readings for all services are taken by the relevant authorities either at completion or very shortly thereafter. The purchaser will need to contact the relevant authorities to make sure that supplies or services are not disconnected. Certain authorities may require a large deposit, usually where directors of the vendor company are re-employed in the same capacity by the purchaser and where the authorities rank as creditors in any insolvency of the vendor company.

If the purchaser is taking over any assets subject to finance agreements, the insolvency practitioner will probably inform the relevant finance companies that he has no further responsibility for such assets from the time of completion. The purchaser will need to make appropriate arrangements with these finance companies as soon as possible, together with any other third party who owns assets needed by the purchaser in the business and which are situated on the company's premises.

In the heat of completion, it has been known for the purchaser to ignore the question of insurance, particularly where the business is being acquired from an insolvency practitioner. The purchaser must not assume that he can take over existing insurances. Most insolvency practitioners will have discontinued any previous insurance cover at the time of their appointment and substituted their own. This insurance cover is terminated with effect from the completion of the sale contract and the purchaser must make suitable alternative arrangements immediately, especially where simultaneous exchange and completion takes place.

Following the acquisition of a business as a going concern from an insolvency practitioner, the sale contract will usually give the purchaser access to certain specific records, such as a list of customers and suppliers, together with a general right to inspect the company's other books and records for a period of time. The purchaser should be aware that whatever general rights he may have been granted, they may be worthless once all the books and records have been bundled into unnamed boxes or plastic sacks for storage, apart from any which have been removed by the insolvency practitioner. Immediately after completion, the purchaser should go through all of the books and records of the previous company, with a representative of the insolvency practitioner, sorting the paperwork and records into:

- company records that the purchaser is entitled to under the sale agreement
- documents which the purchaser may find useful and which are not required by either the insolvency practitioner or the vendor company, such as trade price lists and other literature
- company records which are required by the insolvency practitioner
- company records which remain the responsibility of the directors of the old company or of the liquidator as and when one is appointed
- other paperwork which should be thrown out and destroyed

The purchaser must make sure that he immediately extracts, or reviews, any information he wants, and which is permitted under the sale agreement, from the company records that he is not allowed to retain.

General strategy

Now that he has acquired a company in trouble, the purchaser may find that his problems have only just begun. These problems should be mitigated to a large extent by the investigation process which should have identified the underlying causes of the company's difficulties and given some indication of the changes which would be required.

The results of the investigation should enable the purchaser to prepare a general campaign strategy for the immediate post-acquisition period. At this stage the plan can only be couched in general terms and it will gradually be refined as the purchaser becomes more involved with the new business. The most important decision the purchaser has to make is to identify the individual who is going to manage the post-acquisition business. Hopefully he will have identified this person before the investigation and made him part of the investigation team.

No matter whether the company has been acquired prior to a formal insolvency or as a going concern from an insolvency practitioner, the general post-acquisition strategy of the purchaser will fall into three phases.

- **Phase one** will cover all the immediate, emergency problems which face the purchaser in the early stages. It will inevitably cover a certain amount of crisis management although, after a thorough pre-acquisition investigation, the purchaser should be able to anticipate most of the problems.
- **Phase two** will consist of implementing the fundamental changes required in order to put the company onto a firm business footing. This phase can only be started after the company's immediate problems have been sorted out and after the purchaser has had a chance to assess the situation fully.
- **Phase three** will follow the successful implementation of phases one and two and should be a period of growth and prosperity for the company.

The rest of this chapter will deal with some of the problems which the purchaser is likely to encounter during the first phase of the post-acquisition strategy. There is a wealth of published literature about phases two and three and the purchaser should also take advice from his professional advisors.

Immediately after the acquisition, the purchaser's key priority is to take control of the business. This may mean the introduction of a suitable management information system, or modifying the existing system, so that key financial data can be provided on a daily or weekly basis. This key financial data should include:

- cash position
- new orders received
- sales
- production

- stock levels
- overtime worked
- level of purchase orders
- debtors and creditors position

In the longer term, the purchaser needs to review the compatibility of the management information system with that of any new parent company or group, but this should not be an immediate priority.

At the same time the purchaser needs to restore confidence in the new company with all interested parties. These interested parties may include:

- employees
- trade unions
- suppliers
- customers
- banks

The purchaser should write to all the customers and suppliers of the new company informing them about the acquisition and setting out the purchaser's plans for the future. Key customers and suppliers should be visited personally but the purchaser should avoid making any rash promises at this stage. He should simply inform the parties of the changes which have already occurred and that further changes may take place in the future.

The purchaser should deal carefully with the employees of the acquired company. They are likely to have had a very unsettling period prior to the acquisition and especially during the administration of any insolvency. The purchaser should ensure that all dealings with the employees are both firm and fair and that they are kept fully informed, as appropriate, about the future prospects of the company.

The purchaser needs to assess the future staffing requirements of the company, even if a much reduced workforce has been acquired after an insolvency. If further redundancies are required, the purchaser should try to ensure that these are all made at the same time, as far as possible, in order to minimise any loss of morale on those remaining. The purchaser may also need to inform any unions involved about any possible redundancies.

During the initial period, the purchaser should be assessing any management who have been acquired with the company and appropriate changes should be made. Following a formal insolvency, key employees may have left either prior to or during the insolvency and these will need to be replaced. The purchaser should have obtained details of those employees who were dismissed during the insolvency so that, if necessary, they can be contacted and interviewed by the purchaser, with a view possibly to re-employing them.

In all likelihood, one of the main areas that lacked adequate control in the previous company was the company's level of overheads. This could have been one of the principal factors contributing to the company's troubles. If the purchaser is fortunate, the insolvency practitioner will have already eliminated much of the superfluous overhead expenditure. If not, and particularly as the business begins to recover, the purchaser needs to keep a tight grip on such areas as general administration expenses, motor expenses and expenditure on travel and entertaining among others.

If the insolvency practitioner has cut back on overheads and employees, it will probably have been at the expense of the company's trading. No matter how efficient the insolvency practitioner has been in carrying on the business of the company during the insolvency, the company will probably have lost a certain amount of its customer base during this time, particularly if the insolvency has been a long one. The purchaser's main aim will be to try to recover these lost sales or customers. He can then concentrate on building up the turnover of the company, at the same time as maintaining, or ideally increasing, the profitability.

If the purchaser has acquired all the fixed assets and stock of the previous company, he should carefully review these with a view to disposing of any surplus. It is probably preferable to dispose of any surplus as soon as possible, and to take a reduction in the price, rather than concentrate efforts on obtaining the best possible price at the expense of more important issues.

Debtors and creditors present additional cash flow problems. There are likely to be two principal problems arising from debtors. First, in the case of an acquisition of only the business and assets of a company, the purchaser will have no income from credit sales in the initial period until the first customers of the new business have paid. This initial cash flow deficiency is often forgotten about or, at least, underestimated by purchasers in such circumstances and it is also another sound reason for realising any surplus assets as soon as possible in order to generate cash. Second, the purchaser may have to address a variety of difficulties concerning the actual collection of the new debtors. The company may have had no credit control function or, if it did exist, the company's troubles may have led to an ineffective control of debtors, and the bad habits may have stuck.

These potential difficulties need to be addressed as soon as possible. In addition the purchaser may consider making the sales team responsible, at least in part, for debtor collections, with this role being the principal determining factor for commissions received.

As far as creditors are concerned, the purchaser should be able to obtain credit from all of the suppliers to the previous company, provided that it can clearly be shown that there is no direct connection with the previous company. Problems may be encountered initially, however, where the new company follows on from a previous insolvency. The insolvency practitioner is likely to have been trading on a cash basis with suppliers during the administration of the insolvency and, indeed, the previous company may have had such terms forced upon it for a period prior to the formal insolvency. In the beginning, therefore, the purchaser may find that cash, or proforma, terms will be suggested by at least some of the suppliers, until appropriate credit facilities can be established.

If the purchaser has already carried out a proper investigation, he will probably have identified most of the possible causes of the company's troubles. His first priority will be to stem the losses being incurred by the company from these problem areas. This may simply be a matter of increasing the company's turnover or having reduced bank borrowings, and hence interest charges, but the problems are likely to be more extensive.

The purchaser may discover that the business simply cannot become profitable within its existing framework and that fundamental changes are required in the products or services which are being supplied. Maybe certain lines will need to be deleted or new ones added, or the company will need to redefine its marketplace. Fundamental changes such as these should not be implemented immediately, no matter how tempting this may be for the purchaser. Any changes which are eventually made should result from a carefully researched and deliberated plan.

The middle management and other employees who have been taken over by the purchaser can sometimes offer advice on the company's future strategy. These personnel are likely to have been far better informed about the company's various problems than the directors and other senior management had realised. They may have profitable ideas which could assist the purchaser and which were either never asked for, or ignored, by the previous owners of the business.

Eventually the purchaser will hopefully survive the crises of the first phase of the new company and he will be able to put together a detailed plan to see the company through the second phase, to subsequent growth and prosperity.

Finally, the purchaser should be aware that it is not an easy task to acquire a company in trouble and then not only to stem the losses which have been incurred in the past, but also to achieve an acceptable return on the capital invested in the acquisition. The task will probably take very much longer than originally anticipated and will be considerably more troublesome.

If, after a reasonable period of time, the acquisition is clearly not a success, the purchaser should consider getting out while the going is good. Sufficient may then be salvaged from the company to encourage another acquisition. Otherwise he may have another company in trouble on his hands.

Key point summary

- The purchaser should resolve all residual problems arising directly from the acquisition as soon as possible.
- The purchaser should have identified the individual who is going to manage the new company after the acquisition.
- The purchaser should prepare a plan for the post-acquisition strategy based upon information obtained during the investigation.
- The purchaser should carefully assess the way forward for the new company before introducing any fundamental changes.

Appendix 1: Investigation checklist

Companies House

Obtain search from Companies House and obtain copies of:

- Memorandum and Articles of Association
- Last annual return
- Register of Charges
- Last filed accounts

General review of business and operations

- How and when was the business first set up
- When was the company incorporated
- What changes in ownership have there been since incorporation
- What is the current authorised and issued share capital of the company
- Who are the current officers and shareholders
- What is the structure of the group (if any)
- What was the nature of the original business and what changes have taken place since then
- What is the general geographical area of operations of the company
- What is the nature of the current trade of the company and what are the principal products
- What future changes are contemplated by the management of the company
- Determine whether or not the business of the company is dependent upon a high level of research and development

- Prepare a brief review of the industry sector in which the company operates and comment upon whether or not the market place is growing or declining
- Obtain details of the company's main competitors with an analysis of respective market shares if possible
- Discuss with management about any new markets or sectors which could be entered
- Assess the corporate strategy of the company and whether or not corporate objectives are set by the company's management
- Discuss with directors and management the likely reasons for the company's difficulties
- Analyse the principal strengths and weaknesses of the company
- Detail any possible benefits (for both the purchaser and the target) which are likely to arise out of the proposed acquisition

Previous performance

- Analyse sales by product and market for the last three years
- Highlight sales trends whether seasonal or otherwise
- Detail other income, such as management fees, investment income, rents received, etc.
- Analyse cost of sales (by product and by market if available) between labour, materials and overheads
- Analyse gross profits (by product and by market if possible), calculate gross profit percentages and note any trends
- Review costing procedures
- Obtain copies, and review accuracy, of management accounts
- Analyse overhead expenditure, particularly interest charges, and note any significant trends
- Calculate the company's break-even point
- Analyse any major increases or decreases in balance sheet items over the last three years, at least for such items as:

    - fixed assets (by category)
    - stock and work in progress
    - debtors
    - trade creditors
    - bank overdrafts
    - long-term funding
    - revaluation reserves

- Review depreciation policies

Accounting systems

- Detail the basic accounting systems being used
- Note the involvement of any outside agency such as payroll bureau

- Note any recent changes in the accounting systems or in the staff involved with such systems
- Review the completeness of the accounting systems and how current is the information which is produced. Pay particular attention to:
  - sales ledger
  - purchase ledger
  - accruals for 'other' liabilities
  - 'statutory' returns such as VAT and PAYE
- Note any experience of breakdowns or other problems associated with the accounting systems
- Note the stage to which company staff prepare accounting records

Accounting information

- Enquire as to what information is prepared on a regular basis
- Who produces this information and to whom is it made available
- Obtain copies of the accounting information for relevant periods

Company forecasts

- Obtain copies of any trading, profit or cash flow forecasts prepared by the company
- Review forecasting procedures and comment upon assumptions used
- Review accuracy of previous forecasts
- Note procedures for the approval of forecasts by the directors
- Note the procedures for monitoring actual performance against forecasts and whether or not revised budgets and forecasts are prepared
- Comment upon the adequacy of current overdraft facilities when compared with forecasts
- Comment on significant matters which may affect forecasts and perform sensitivity analysis

Subsidiaries and other connected companies

- Identify ownership, management, nature and place of business of such companies
- Enquire about reasons for acquisition or connection
- Review intercompany management charges and dividends
- Ascertain whether or not subsidiaries operate independently or through holding company
- Review level of investment and compare with present market values for any subsidiary
- Review any intercompany guarantee arrangements

- Review the nature and content of any intercompany accounts and any reconciliations thereof

Banking arrangements

- Detail bankers and other lenders to both company and any subsidiaries or connected companies
- Obtain details of banking facilities granted (including rates of interest charged) and any security given by the company
- Obtain details of any third-party guarantees such as directors, subsidiaries or other companies
- Review long-term borrowings noting:

  - period of loan
  - dates of repayment
  - interest rates
  - security given

Management

- Identify the person who makes the key decisions in the company
- Obtain a copy of the company's management organisation chart
- Establish the name, age, qualifications, skill or discipline and length of service for all key members of staff or management and prepare brief curriculum vitae as appropriate
- For all key employees, establish remuneration package including benefits in kind and pension arrangements
- Obtain copies of any service agreements
- Establish the reasons for any key personnel who may have left in the previous six months
- Enquire about any key personnel who are expected to leave or to retire in the near future

Employees and staff

- Obtain a summary of the numbers of all employees and staff, other than key personnel, analysed by departments, sex, part-time or full-time, and weekly or monthly paid
- Obtain details of any redundancies in the last six months together with any planned redundancies, broken down as above
- Obtain details of any trade unions recognised by the company together with the following information:

  - name of local representatives both inside and outside the company
  - number of employees in each union

- details of any recent or unresolved problems
- whether there is a closed shop agreement in force

- Obtain, in summary form, details of current rates of pay or salaries, analysed by department
- Obtain details of the most recent, and any imminent, pay awards or wage agreements and establish that any imminent pay awards have been incorporated into the company's forecasts
- Comment upon the general recruitment policy of the company and any training procedures
- Obtain details of any company pension scheme or employee share option scheme
- Obtain details of any shareholders' or directors' relatives who are working for the company together with details of their remuneration packages
- Obtain a summary of any personnel who are not employed under the PAYE scheme, such as agents, salesmen, subcontractors, etc.
- In respect of self-employed personnel, establish whether or not any Inland Revenue procedures to make gross payments are being operated correctly
- Establish the usual methods of calculating pay or bonuses
- Establish for all weekly and monthly paid personnel:

  - the normal and current working hours
  - how wages are paid (such as weekly in arrears)
  - the usual method of payment (such as cash, cheque or bank giro credit)
  - the usual payment days
  - holiday pay arrangements

- Obtain sample contracts of employment
- Obtain details of any welfare services which may be available for employees and staff

Sales and marketing

- Obtain an analysis of sales by product, geographical areas and major customers or customer type, with comparative figures for previous periods
- Prepare a summary of the company's selling and distribution procedures and policies
- Obtain details of any sales team or agents used by the company together with details of remuneration and terms of appointment
- Obtain details of any invoice or debt factoring agreement together with details of any excluded items
- Obtain details of any insurance cover for both export or non-export sales
- Determine the management's future plans for any expansion or contraction of the range of goods or services supplied by the company
- Determine the company's procedures for introducing new product lines and for developing old products
- Determine the bases used for establishing the prices at which goods or services

are sold and the philosophy behind any sales discounts which are offered to customers

- Obtain details of the last price increases and any such imminent increases
- Obtain details of any major sales contracts which are in the course of manufacture
- Obtain details of the company's current order book and prepare a summary thereof
- Discuss with management the effect of new technology, likely competition or other changes in the market place which may affect the company's sales
- Obtain details of any deposits which have been taken from customers together with details of any insurance cover or trust account procedures which are in use in respect of such deposits

Purchasing

- Detail the company's principal suppliers and the raw materials used by the company together with details of any forward purchasing contracts
- Comment upon the price stability of the principal purchases
- Detail any recent major increases in the cost of purchases, whether any such price increases are known to be imminent and whether such increases have been included in the company's forecasts
- Enquire as to whether the company has had to change its principal suppliers in the recent past and whether such changes were instigated internally or externally
- Make enquiries about any difficulties which have been experienced in obtaining supplies in the past and the effect that this has had upon production or sales

Production/work in progress

- Prepare a general description of the manufacturing process
- Determine the company's policy about producing goods to order or for stock
- Enquire as to whether payments on account are obtained from customers for long or major orders
- Determine the basis of the production programme and enquire about procedures for varying the programme
- What is the average production timescale
- Where short production runs are undertaken, what is the down time required to change between different production runs
- Obtain details of any work which is given to outside subcontractors and, in particular, details of the ownership of the tools and dies involved in such work
- Detail any ways in which production is constrained by any seasonal or other variation in orders, availability of raw materials or suitability or reliability of the production machinery or employees

- Enquire about the quality of the production plant and machinery and the company's policy for the replacement thereof
- Enquire about the total capacity of the factory and whether or not there is any scope for increasing capacity
- Detail the company's procedures for measuring both the costs to date on contracts in progress against estimates and the value of work completed to date
- Review the company's policies for taking profit on long-term contracts

Land and buildings

- Obtain precise location details for all of the company's premises including sales offices, distribution depots, warehouses, etc.
- Obtain the following details for each property:

  - general description
  - site area and floor space including any unutilized space
  - any planning approvals or restrictions which may be relevant
  - original cost plus the cost of any additions

- Note the general condition of all company properties
- Obtain copies of any recent professional valuations of the properties
- Enquire about any revaluation of properties which has been included in the statutory accounts
- Obtain copies of any leases granted to the company and schedule principal, relevant terms. In particular, note date when rent was last due and whether or not paid
- Obtain copies of any leases granted by the company and schedule principal terms and rents received
- Enquire whether any informal business tenancies have been granted either by or to the company
- Discuss possible alternative uses for properties
- Establish that the company has legal title to its properties and ascertain whereabouts of title documentation
- Enquire about the sale or purchase of any property which is either in progress or pending
- Review the insurance of all properties
- Enquire about any grants which may have been received in connection with property purchases and the current status of such grants

Plant, machinery, motor vehicles, office furniture and equipment

- Enquire about the existence of any plant register and whether or not it is up to date
- Prepare a summary of the cost and depreciation of relevant assets by appropriate category

- Summarize depreciation rates used for each category of asset
- Enquire about any recent valuation of the assets and ascertain the reason behind any such revaluation and the bases used
- Enquire about any revaluation of assets which has been included in the statutory accounts
- Note the age and condition of the principal assets
- Discuss with management the degree of specialisation of any assets
- Enquire about any significant assets which are on loan either to or from the company
- Enquire about any grants which have been received in connection with the purchase of assets and review any potential liability for the repayment of such grants
- Cross-reference asset schedules with schedules of finance obligations
- Cross-reference company vehicle schedules with schedule of employees and enquire about arrangements for the private use of such vehicles
- Review insurance of assets
- Enquire about significant purchases of assets which are either being contemplated or which would be considered if funds were available

Assets under finance or rental agreements

- Obtain copies of all finance and rental agreements involving company assets
- Prepare a summary of all such agreements grouped by the finance companies concerned and detail for each agreement:

  - description of asset
  - the original purchase price
  - the 'financed' amount
  - the length of the agreement
  - any arrears outstanding under the agreement
  - future amounts payable under the agreement
  - the estimated current value of the asset

- Cross-reference schedule of finance agreements to assets schedules
- Physically inspect principal assets under finance agreements

Intangible assets

- Prepare a schedule of all patents, trade marks, etc., and extract any registration details and the life thereof
- Prepare a schedule of any licence agreements
- Check ownership of any relevant intangible assets
- Discuss any goodwill existing in the books of the company and enquire about how such goodwill arose, its original value and any policy for writing it off

Stocks

- Prepare a summary of all stocks held at each business location, using an appropriate analysis such as raw materials, components, stores and finished goods
- Attempt to identify any slow-moving or obsolete stock and establish company policy for dealing with such stock
- Detail any stocks held which belong to third parties
- Establish the basis for valuing stocks for accounts purposes and check that such a basis has been consistently applied
- Enquire as to how often a physical stock count is undertaken
- Enquire as to the method of ascertaining quantities of stock held
- Review the results of comparing the last physical stock count with the stock records
- Ascertain how up to date the stock records are
- What is the annual rate of stock turnover, analysed by type of product or product group if possible
- Identify the major groups of stock which may be subject to reservation of title claims

Debtors

- Obtain and review the latest aged list of debtors
- Prepare summaries of aged list of debtors in appropriate alternative forms such as:
  - by age, highlighting older debts
  - by size of account
  - by home and export customers
  - by interim invoices, final invoices and retentions where contracts are involved
- Schedule the size and age of all individual major customers
- Schedule the size and age of all individual subsidiary and connected company debtors
- Schedule all debtor balances which are also creditors of the company and determine the amounts involved
- Schedule all major credit balances on the sales ledger, with a summary of the smaller credit balances, and determine the reasons therefore
- Obtain details of the usual terms of credit given by the company for both major customers and customers in general
- Obtain details of the reserves and provisions for bad and doubtful debts
- Review the company's history of bad debts
- Obtain details of any major disputes with debtors
- Review credit notes issued in the last six months and comment upon the frequency and amount of any significant credits or returns
- Establish the nature and extent of any product guarantees or warranties and review the claims within the last six months

- Establish the credit control methods and systems within the company and, in particular, note the department which is responsible for the granting of credit
- Review any customer 'stop' list which exists
- Review the debt collection procedures within the company and establish the extent to which debt collection agencies or solicitors are used
- Where debtors or invoices are factored or discounted, review the reconciliations with the company concerned and establish the reasons for any excluded items
- Review sundry debtors and prepayments
- Check legality, and potential tax liability, of any loans to directors

Cash

- Summarize cash in hand and at bank
- Where cash in hand is significant, check cut-off with bank accounts, debtors, etc.
- Where cash at bank is significant, obtain details of any restrictions on withdrawal and any set-off arrangements with any overdrafts or loans

Investments

- Prepare a schedule of any investments, including details of any holdings, market values and terms of repayment
- Prepare a schedule of any insurance policies held where the company is a beneficiary and obtain surrender values

Preferential creditors

- For all Government preferential creditors, prepare a schedule detailing:
  - the date of the last return
  - the period covered by the return
  - the amount paid

- Schedule all amounts due to preferential creditors up to the date of the investigation
- Establish whether any agreement for the payment of arrears has been reached with any preferential creditor, what payments on account under such an agreement have been made, the dates of such payments and how such payments have been appropriated
- Enquire about the last visits to the company by representatives of any Government department and the outcome of such visits
- Prepare a schedule of amounts due to employees (as at the date of the investigation) in respect of arrears of pay and holiday pay

Other creditors

- Obtain a list of trade and expense creditors of the company (aged if possible) and prepare a summary thereof
- Schedule principal debit balances on the company's purchase ledger and enquire about the reasons therefor
- Obtain details of major suppliers and outstanding balances due to such creditors
- Obtain details of all current balances due to company bankers and other lenders and establish extent of usual items appearing in bank reconciliations, particularly unpresented cheques
- Check to ensure that the company does not follow a policy of raising cheques and then delaying before dispatching them
- Review the company's procedures for goods received but not invoiced and procedures for establishing other accruals
- Obtain details of all other creditors, such as directors' loan accounts and other loans with details of any arrears, repayment terms and interest thereon
- Prepare a summary of any writs, judgements or statutory demands received by the company in the last six months and detail any which are still outstanding
- Enquire as to whether any creditor either has threatened to distrain or levy execution on any assets of the company or has obtained a walking possession order
- Obtain details of any informal meetings or discussions with principal suppliers and the outcome of the same
- Prepare a summary of the potential liability to employees in respect of payments in lieu of notice and redundancy payments

Taxation

- Prepare a schedule of all taxation liabilities and obtain details of any disputed matters
- Obtain details of any reliefs which have not yet been taken or any losses which may be available to carry forward
- Obtain details (from the company's accountants) of the current state of the taxation affairs of the company

Other matters

- Review the general insurance of the company
- Review any pension schemes operated by the company
- Prepare a summary of any transactions with directors
- Review the company's statutory books and minutes of directors' and shareholders' meetings and obtain explanations about any unusual matters contained therein

- Recheck the company's file at Companies House to ensure that all relevant documents have been filed

Conclusion

- Prepare written investigation report

Appendix 2: Proforma statement of estimated financial position

ABC COMPANY LIMITED

Statement of estimated financial position as at 30 June 1991

	Audited accounts as at 31 December 1990		Estimated book values as at 30 June 1991		Estimated realisable values			
					Going concern basis		Forced sale basis	
	£'000	£'000	£'000	£'000	£'000	£'000	£'000	£'000
ASSETS SUBJECT TO FIXED CHARGE								
Leasehold warehouse		120		110		75		75
Freehold factory and offices	512		517		675		625	
Less 1st mortgage	(159)		(155)		(155)		(155)	
		353		362		520		470
Trade and sundry debtors		514		539		475		350
Investment in subsidiary		49		26		–		–
		1 036		1 037		1 070		820
Less secured by fixed charge:								
Barminster Bank plc		(692)		(855)		(855)		(855)
Surplus/(deficiency) carried down		344		182		215		(35)
ASSETS SUBJECT TO FLOATING CHARGE								
Plant and machinery	346		327		294		201	
Motor vehicles	126		111		100		95	
Less hire purchase and leasing obligations	(154)		(129)		(129)		(129)	
	318		309		265		167	
Stock	498		356		340		94	
Work in progress	196		193		140		17	
Office furniture and equipment	29		25		15		8	
Prepaid expenses	19		7		7		–	
		1 060		890		767		286
PREFERENTIAL CREDITORS								
Inland Revenue – PAYE and NIC	(49)		(54)		(54)		(54)	
Customs and Excise – VAT	(27)		(48)		(48)		(48)	
Employees – arrears of pay and holiday pay	(69)		(125)		(125)		(125)	
	(145)		(227)		(227)		(227)	
		915		663		540		59
DEBENTURE HOLDER								
Barminster Bank plc – balance brought down		344		182		215		(35)
		1 259		845		755		24
UNSECURED CREDITORS								
Trade and expense creditors	(296)		(375)		(375)		(375)	
Accruals	(24)		(37)		(37)		(37)	
Outstanding cheques	(54)		(69)		(69)		(69)	
Directors' loan accounts	(75)		(120)		(120)		(120)	
Other unsecured loans	(75)		(70)		(70)		(70)	
Employees – lieu of notice and redundancy payments	–		–		–		(124)	
		(524)		(671)		(671)		(795)
NET ASSETS/(LIABILITIES)		735		174		84		(771)
SHARE CAPITAL		(5)		(5)		(5)		(5)
TOTAL ESTIMATED SURPLUS/(DEFICIENCY)		730		169		79		(776)

Index

Accountants
  as acquisitions advisors, 41, 43–4
  and administrative receivership, 23–4
  information from, 7, 8
Accounts
  information from, 13, 55–9, 118
  ownership of books of, 107–8, 111–12
  problems with use of, 15–16
  systems of, 57, 117–18
Acquisition see Buying a company
Actuaries, 45
Administration order, 25–6, 101
Administrative receivership, 23–4, 26, 38,
  101
Advertising, 7, 93–4
Advisors in buying a company, 40–46
Altman's Z score, 13
Appointment, validity of, 100–101
Assets
  decrease in, and company failure, 13
  disclosure of, in contracts, 102–4
  and finance agreements, 64–5, 72–4, 111
  hidden, of companies in trouble, 2–3
  investigation and valuation of, 10–11, 19,
    24, 51, 63–9, 121–4
  and reservation of title, 74–6
  in statement of affairs, 50–53
Asset-strippers, 3
Auctions, 93, 95, 96
Audit report, qualification of, 13

Auditors
  as acquisition advisors, 42–3
  change of, and company failure, 13
Autocratic management, 15

Bailiffs, 11, 49
Banks
  advice on acquisitions from, 45
  appointment of investigating
    accountants by, 23, 24
  change of, and company failure, 13
  credit facilities from, 9–10, 13
  and finance of acquisition, 87–8
  information from, 7
  of target company, 59, 119
Books and records, 107–8, 111–12
Borrowing see Finance
Buildings see Property
Business brokers, 7
Business plan, 3–5, 87, 112–15
Business sector surveys, 7
Businesses and Assets, 7
Buying a company
  advisors on, 40–46
  after insolvency, 37–9, 48–9
  contract for, 99–109
  finance of, 87–8
  investigations before, 47–53
    guidelines on, 54–71, 116–27
  methods of, 91–3

negotiation of, 89–98
post-completion matters and, 4, 108, 110–15
prior to insolvency, 35–7, 49
problems after, 45–6
reuse of name after, 84–6

Cash holdings, 69, 125
Cash-flow, 58, 114
'Caveat emptor' clauses, 104–5
Commission payments, 68
Completion of sale, 108–9
Compulsory liquidation, 22, 26
Confidentiality clauses, 108
Connected (subsidiary) companies, 6, 58–9, 118–19
Contingent liabilities, 10
Contract debtors, 68
Contracts: for buying a business, 99–109
Cork, Sir Kenneth, 28
Corporate voluntary arrangements, 26
Costing systems, 16, 56
Costs, control of, 17, 113–14
Credit agencies, 12
Credit control, 17, 68
Credit facilities
    from banks, 9–10,13
    inappropriate use of, 17
Credit notes, 67–8
Creditors' 10, 51, 52, 69–70, 114, 125–6
Creditors' voluntary liquidation, 20–22, 26
Crisis management, 10
Customers
    investigation of, 61, 67
    large, overreliance on, 16–17
    loss of reputation with, 14
    post-completion stage and, 113, 114
Customs and Excise, 10, 69, 107, 110

Debenture holders, 23, 24, 25
Debt factoring, 61
Debtors, 67–9, 114, 124–5
Department of Employment, 80, 81
Department of Social Security, 69
Department of Trade and Industry, 27, 28, 29
Deposits
    from customers, 61
    to insolvency practitioners, 97
Directors
    attempts to obtain funds by, 6–7
    as debtors, 68
    disqualification of, 28–30
    evidence on companies from, 47–8, 70
    information about, 55
    and liquidation, 20–23
    problems with, as cause of failure, 14–15

re-employment of, 85, 86–7
Directory of Authorised Insolvency Practitioners, 27
Discount schemes, 61, 62
Distraints, 70
Distribution problems, 17
Diversification, 15
Dutch auction, 96

Employees
    investigation of, 60–61, 119–20
    labilities to, 69, 70, 78–9, 108
        in insolvency situations, 79–83
    in post-completion stage, 113, 115
    turnover of, 14
    see also directors; managers; sales force
Employment, Department of, 80, 81
Expansion, plans for, 3, 4

Factoring, 61
Failure see Insolvency
Finance
    for acquisition of companies, 87–8
    from banks, 9–10, 13
    inappropriate use of, 17
Finance agreements, 64–5, 72–4, 111, 123
Financial control, problems with, 15–16
Financial Times, 7, 94
Fixed assets see Assets
Forced sale valuation, 90
Forecasts, 58, 118
Fraudulent trading, 30
Funding see Finance

Going concern valuation, 90
Goodwill, 24, 65, 84, 86
Groups of companies, 6, 58–9, 118–19
Guarantors for a contract, 101–2

Hire purchase, 13, 64–5, 72–4

Inappropriate funding, 17
In-house acquisition team, 41–2
Inland Revenue, 10, 61, 69, 110
Insolvency (failure)
    buying a company after, 37–9
    definitions of, 10, 18–19
    process of, 9–12
    reasons for, 14–18
    signs of, 12–14
    types of, 20–26
Insolvency accountants, 43–4
Insolvency practitioners, 20, 26, 27–8, 48
    contracts with, 99–109
    and disqualification of directors, 29
    and employees of companies, 79–83

and finance agreements, 72–3
investigations by, 11–12
and name of company, 84
negotiation with, 93–8
and reservation of title, 74–6
Insurance, 61, 111
Insurance bonds, 28
Intangible assets, 65, 123
Intellectual property, 65
Intercompany accounts, 58–9
Intercompany guarantees, 6, 59
Investment(s)
dangers of, 6–7
investigation of, 69, 125
Invoice factoring, 61

Journals, information from, 7

Land see Property
Leased assets, 13, 63, 64–5, 72–4, 106
License agreements, 65
Liquidation, 20–23, 26, 30
Litster case, 81, 82
Loan capital, 15
Loaned assets, 77

Machinery (plant), 17, 45, 64, 122–3
Mail, redirection of, 110–11
Management accounts, 10, 16, 56, 57–8
Managers
buy-outs by, 2, 8
negotiation with, and purchase of
company, 48, 56, 60, 94, 119
and post-completion stage, 4, 113, 115
problems with, and company failure,
14–15
quality of, 5
Managing director, autocratic, 15
Market share, loss of, 14
Marketing strategy, investigation of, 61,
120–21
Media see Press
Members' voluntary liquidation, 23
Merchant banks, 7
Motor vehicles, 64, 65, 122–3

Name of a company, reuse of, 84–6
National Insurance, 69
Negotiation procedures, 89–98

Office equipment, 64, 122–3
Overdrafts, 9–10
Overtrading, 18

Patent agents, 45
Patents, 65

Pension schemes, 45, 60
Plant and machinery, 17, 45, 64, 122–3
Post Office, 110–11
Post-completion matters, 4, 108, 110–15
Preferential creditors, 69, 125
Press and other media
information from, 7, 93–4
statements to, 108
Private treaty sale, 93
Produce Marketing Consortium Ltd, 30–31
Production
investigation of, 62–3, 121–2
problems with, 18
Profit projections, 58
Profitability, decline in, 9–10, 13
Property
in contracts, 105–6
investigation of, 63, 122
Property agents, 44–5
Purchase see Buying a company

Receivership, administrative, 23–4, 26, 38,
101
Recessions, 15
Records and books, 107–8, 111–12
Redundancies, 80, 113
Rented assets, 77, 123
Reputation, loss of, 14
Reservation of title, 74–6
Restrictive trading agreement, 100
Romalpa clause, 74

Sale see Buying a company
Sale of Goods Act (1979), 74
'Sale or return' agreements, 77
Sales
forecasts of, 58
investigation of, 61, 120–21
Sales force
commission to, 68
problems with, 17
Self-employment, 61
Sensitivity analysis, 58
Services and utilities, 111
Shadow directors, 28
Shareholders: and liquidation, 20–21
Shares, purchase of, 33–4, 91–2
Social Security, Department of, 69
Solicitors, 1–2, 42, 44, 99
Staff see Employees
Statement of Affairs, 24, 50–53, 129
Stationery, 110
Statutory accounts, 13, 55–6
Statutory demands, 11, 70

Stock
   control of, 66
   levels of, 17–18
   valuation of, 62, 66–7, 124
Stock takers, 45
Strategic business plan, 3–5, 87, 112–15
Subcontractors, 62
Subsidiary companies, 6, 58–9, 118–19
Suppliers
   investigation of, 61–2, 121
   overreliance on, 16–17
   post-completion stage and, 113, 114

Taxation, 69, 70–71, 107, 110, 126
Tender sale, 93
Third party assets, 72–7, 111
Title, reservation of, 74–6
Trade associations, 7
Trade and Industry, Department of, 27, 28, 29
Trade mark agents, 45
Trade marks, 65
Trading forecasts, 58
Transactions at undervalue, 31–2

Transfer of Undertakings (Protection of Employment) Regulations (1981), 80
Turnover, 13

Undervalue, transactions at, 31–2
Unfair dismissal, 81–2
Unsecured creditors, 70, 126
Utilities and services, 111

Validity of appointment, 100–101
Value added tax, 69, 107, 111
Vehicles, 64, 65, 122–3
Voluntary liquidations, 20–22, 23, 26

Walking possession orders, 70
Welfab Engineers Ltd, 37
Winding-up petitions, 11, 12, 49, 70
Work in progress, 62–3, 121–2
Workers *see* Employees
Writs, 11, 12, 70
Wrongful trading, 30

Z score, 13